PRAISE FOR ULTRASONIC

Grand and active listening requires real engagement and unexpected risks. In Steven Church's thoroughly alive compendium, the act of listening itself has the power to create identity, lead inward towards irrevocable grief and awe, and outward into the ever-curious world. How "ultra" in its sonic musings can a mind be? Church's intense soundscape considers subjects as ranging as racquetball, idleness, and firefighting, as poetic as word-origins, and as ancient as birth, love, and loss.

—Lia Purpura, author of *Rough Likeness* and *On Looking*

Each beautifully crafted essay in Steven Church's *Ultrasonic* invites the reader into an intriguing new world. From Elvis playing racquetball to the drumming heartbeat of an infant to prehistoric bottom feeders, Church's endless curiosity and wildly intelligent prose pierce the literary bull's-eye, spot on.

—Dinty W. Moore, author of *Between Panic & Desire*

If Montaigne were a mad cartographer driven to find the true unnamable intersection of earth and human body, with a heart the size of the sun, he would have looked something like Steven Church. The collection begins as a meditation on the ways in which we use sound to draw chalk outlines around the things we can see only incompletely, and then becomes so much more than that—one of the oddest and loveliest meditations on parenthood I've ever read. I love this book beyond reason, and I love it beyond whatever reason's opposite is too.

—Matthew Gavin Frank, author
Concerning the Giant Squid and It

Steven Church has spent the past decade quietly becoming one of our best essayists, and I've been eagerly awaiting the book containing these deeply resonant essays. By turns humorous, reflective, curious, mischievous, and profound, *Ultrasonic* gives booming confirmation: Church's is a voice we should all listen to.

—**Patrick Madden**, author of *Quotidiana*

Like Elvis Presley's legendarily fierce final match on the Graceland racquetball court, these essays ricochet, they zing, they demand our attention. Steven Church's spinning insights often come with lightning quickness—surprise attacks buried in graceful delivery—but his approach is so welcoming I found myself rising back to my feet for return service at every paragraph. Readers who fancy a bout of lively and uncompromising nonfiction will find a worthy opponent in these nimble inquiries about sound, tricks of memory, limitations of the body, and the varied perils of American manhood.

—**Elena Passarello,** author of *Let Me Clear My Throat*

Steven Church writes with the virtuosic intelligence and digressive curiosity of Montaigne, but beneath the desk his feet are planted firmly on a double bass kick drum. These essays rumble and crack with percussive thunder; they thrum with music and rhythm; like the best heavy metal or rap, they kickstart the heart muscle. With equal parts tenderness and rage, Church tunnels through our noise-laden culture to locate a clear signal: it's empathy—for our children, our neighbors, our fellow humans. I can't think of another collection that has moved me so deeply on both sensory and emotional levels. *Ultrasonic* is a tale told by a literary mastermind, full of sound and fury, signifying everything.

—**Justin Hocking,** author of *The Great Floodgates of the Wonderworld*

ULTRASONIC

(Essays)

Steven Church

Lavender Ink
New Orleans
lavenderink.org

Ultrasonic

Published in New Orleans by Lavender Ink.

Copyright © 2014 by Steven Church and Lavender Ink.

ISBN: 978-1935084-70-9

Other editions:
Ebook: 978-1935084-71-6

Cover Design: Kristen Radtke
Book design: Bill Lavender

PUBLICATION ACKNOWLEDGEMENTS

The author gratefully acknowledges those literary journals, sites, and anthologies that previously published the essays in this book.

"Auscultation," appeared originally in *The Pedestrian*, Fall 2010, and was reprinted in the *2011 Best American Essays*.

"Ultrasonic," appeared originally in *Fourth Genre*, Fall 2009.

"All of a Dither," appeared originally in *AGNI*, Fall 2010.

"Seven Fathoms Down," appeared originally in issue 13.5 of *DIAGRAM*, Fall 2013.

"Bird Watching in Fresno," appeared originally in *Wag's Review*, 2009, and was reprinted in YOU: An Anthology of Essays Dedicated to the 2nd Person (Welcome Table Press), 2013.

"Crown and Shoulder," appeared originally in *Passages North*, 2014.

"Lag Time," appeared originally in *Brevity* #33, 2010.

"On Loitering," appeared originally in *The Rumpus*, May 2013, and a revised version will be reprinted as, "On Idleness" in the anthology *After Montaigne: Contemporary Essayists Cover The Essays*, University of Georgia Press, 2015.

"It Begins with a Knock at the Door," appeared originally as "Confessions of a Parasite," in the 2010 *Sonora Review*.

"Playlist for Finishing a Book," appeared originally in a different form as part of the "Book Notes" series on the *Largehearted Boy* music/literature blog in Spring, 2010.

SOUNDINGS

ULTRASONIC

(ESSAYS)

Author's Note

Sounding as an adjective means *sonorous* or *resonant*. It booms, all echo and reverberation. But sounding also refers to *the act of measuring depth with a sounding line*, unspooling a thread until it drags bottom. And it is also *that depth ascertained*, the thing itself. It is action and record. And to take a sounding is *to measure atmospheric conditions at different heights*, to test the weather of a particular place, a physical landscape; and it is *a probe, a test, a sampling of opinion*. In this book, essays become sounding lines, explorations, probes and tests, each one a map of what lies below the surface; and the form is meant to mimic the way our thinking sometimes moves between points of engagement—navigating in the dark by means of echolocation, bouncing from one idea to another, searching and seeing through sound. – SC

FOR MY MOTHER, SALLY RAMAGE

AUSCULTATION

CHAMBER 1

In August 2007, a few months before my second child, a daughter, was born, the entire country waited to hear news of six miners trapped fifteen hundred feet underground by a massive cave-in at the Crandall Canyon coal mine in Utah. The catastrophic collapse was so intense that it registered as a 3.9 magnitude earthquake on local seismographs. Rescuers began the arduous three-day process of digging the men out. They installed seismic listening devices on the surface and set off three dynamite charges, a signal to any surviving miners to make noise. Lots of noise. The electronic ears listened for the sound of hammers pounding on the rock and on roof bolts, the telltale rap-and-thump of human life. They listened and listened but never heard a thing.

Six miners missing. Six boreholes drilled into different areas of the mine. They sent oxygen sensors, cameras, and microphones down through PVC pipe, fishing in each hole, searching every possible area for the men. Oxygen levels were misread, confused, and, ultimately, determined to be dangerously low. Three rescue workers trying to dig the trapped miners out were also killed when a wall of the mine "exploded" and crushed them. No sign was ever heard of the miners, and all six men were considered missing and presumed dead. All rescue efforts were eventually abandoned. I don't know if there is a signal for this, another series of blasts to say good-bye, or some other ceremonial end to the search. Maybe they just switch off the drills and unplug their ears.

The owner of the mine, Bob Murray, held a press conference and said, "Had I known that this evil mountain, this alive mountain, would do what it did, I would never have sent the miners in here. I'll never go near that mountain again."

Finally, a seventh hole was bored into the mountain and through this hole they pumped thousands of gallons of mud and debris, filling all remaining cavities and sealing the tomb off permanently with the missing miners still inside.

Researchers at Utah State University and other places have been working to create more effective listening and noise-making devices to help trapped miners—some of them seemingly crude and simplistic, yet still effective. One plan calls for 4X4 inch iron plates to be placed at regular intervals in the tunnels with sledgehammers kept nearby—the idea being that a trapped miner can find his way to a station and slam the hammer into the iron plate over and over again. Think of the noise below. Think of your ears. Geophones on the surface—the kind of sensors they use to anticipate earthquakes—would register the sound waves created by the hammer pings and create a listening grid, a virtual sound map of the mine. They would then use the map to pinpoint the exact location of any miners still kicking below the earth's rugged crust.

CHAMBER 2

Recall the ice cold press of the metal disc against your chest cavity, the sting and soft burn as it warms on your clavicle, your breastbone, fingers moving metal across your naked chest, around behind, fingertips stepping down your spine, one hand on your hip, maybe your shoulder, the other sliding around your rib cage, always always with the whispered command, *breathe . . . breathe . . . good*, and the eyes staring not at you but at the cold diaphragm, the metallic spot moving across your body, listening as if your body possesses a voice of its own and speaks in a language only the doctor understands. The metal diaphragm only broadcasts its secret to the trained ear. When it touches you, it knows you. It sings sounds of your body, noises you can barely imagine—the hypnotic pump of organs, the soft ebb and flow of blood in your veins, and the breathy whisper of lungs at work—noises that can name you *normal*, *healthy*, or *not*. The intimate instrument—the stethoscope—knows your body in a way your own hands and ears never will.

Chamber 3

Some heart doctors train their ears on classical music—Mozart and Bach and Chopin—learning to discern the individual instruments. They learn to listen for the flaws and failings of the heart, train to recognize the music of machine-like muscle efficiency, and understand when a noise is a bad noise. They depend on the stethoscope for more than diagnoses. They need the tool to complete the image. Nothing promises "Doctor" like the stethoscope draped around an exposed neck or curled over a pressed, collared shirt, perhaps tucked neatly into the pocket of a white lab coat, or clutched firmly in hand, authoritatively like a hammer, a plumber's seat wrench, a scalpel—the only tool for an specific job. You know the flexible latex tubing, the chrome-plated ear tubes, the hard metal diaphragm—cold, round, smooth as pearl, reflective as a mirror. The stethoscope immediately defines "doctor"—the promise of care and pain management, a reliquary of body knowledge, someone you trust with your life. Think of the things you've allowed another person to do and say to you—mainly because he or she wore the uniform of doctor, mainly because that person carried a stethoscope. We don't check résumés or credentials, don't ask for service reviews or certificates. We expect the object—even if it's never used (but it's always used). Its touch conjures sense memory, too—that repeated sweet burn pressed to your flesh. Regardless of physical context or attire (say at a crowded beach, on a subway, or a mountain trail) the stethoscope speaks. It says, "I am a medical professional," and in so doing it grants rights and responsibilities, obligations and expectations. It tells us you will do no harm. It tells us you know what you are talking about. Every child's doctor play set comes with a plastic stethoscope because you can't even adequately pretend to be a doctor without one.

As object, the stethoscope functions as both necessarily and sufficient condition of "Doctorness." But this identity and image—of the doctor as listener, as diviner of significant sounds through a stethoscope, the magician of auscultation—is a relatively new one, just over 150 years old. The French doctor, René Laënnec is credited by many for inventing the first stethoscope, or at least introducing the diagnostic practice of auscultation. In a paper published in 1819, he says:

> I was consulted by a young woman with symptoms of a diseased heart...percussion was of little avail on account ...of fatness. The application of the ear... inadmissible by the age and sex of the patient. I recollected a fact in acoustics ... the augmented sound conveyed through solid bodies....I rolled a quire of paper into a cylinder and applied one end to the heart and one end to the ear...and thereby perceived the action of the heart...more clear and distinct. I have been enabled to discover new signs of the diseases of the lungs, heart and pleura.[1]

It wasn't until the 1851 invention by Arthur Leared and the refinement in 1852 by George Cammann of the binaural stethoscope—a simple but incredibly significant instrument—that the practice of refined auscultation began to develop and doctors could listen in stereo to the sounds of the body. Before that it was a crude monaural amplifying horn, Laënnec's ear trumpet, which offered little more than a distant thump against the rib cage. Without binaural stethoscope technology, auscultation was more like listening for trees falling in distant forests or for the faint tapping of a trapped miner. But doctors still pressed ears to chest cavities and listened for the pings, trying to read the heart

---

1   Harry Bloch, "The Inventor of the Stethoscope: Rene Laennec" *Journal of Family Practice*, 31 Mar, 2010.

noises and tremors. L. A. Conner (1867-1950), the founder of the American Heart Association, is said to have carried a silk handkerchief to place on the chest of a patient when he practiced ear auscultation and diagnosis.[2]

For 100 years, cardiologists relied on Cammann's binaural scope to detect the slightest abnormality: arrhythmia, skip, hop, hammer, block, or stutter. 1952 and 1964 saw further refinements of the traditional binaural stethoscope, with many cardiologists believing that the now all-but-obsolete Rapport-Sprague was the finest auscultation device ever made or used, allowing them unprecedented clarity and consistency.

Current auscultation practice often employs an electronic stethoscope, which is not actually a listening device but a noise translator that generates a reproduction of the heartbeat, bullying the human ear out of it's place as the direct register of the heart. The doctor isn't listening to the heart directly but to a digital translation of the heart's sounds.

I heard the *whoosh-whoosh* of my daughter's heart first as reproduction, electronic transmission through a fetal heart monitor strapped to my wife's belly—a type of electronic stethoscope. The sound is less a *thump* than a *slosh*. More valve and flap than muscled push. But it is still a treasured sound. For most of our prenatal visits, medical intervention extended only as far as placement of the fetal heart monitor. The first thing we did—doctor and parents—was listen. All together. We awaited the news of life. And anyone who's been in this place understands the simple comfort of that sound, the reassurance of noise—or more specifically, the doctor's recognition that this is *normal* noise.

---

2   Ibid.

A baby's heartbeat is the first sensory experience a father has with his child, often the first moment that a father begins to think of the fetus as a child, a baby with body and brain and lungs and a drumming heart. First identity. The first hint of possibility filtered through an electronic translator, reproduced from a tiny speaker. But still, nothing promises person like these first heart sounds. Nothing says, *it begins*, like the *wish-wish-wish* noise of the stubborn pump—and I say this with both knowledge and ignorance of the ethical implications for some.

Perhaps because of facts, stats, opinions and ideas, perhaps because I had no other way to feel each of my wife's pregnancies before the heartbeat, fatherhood was mostly an abstraction. I never really began to *feel* like the baby's father until I heard the thumping inside, that telltale sound of life; or perhaps my son was not a son, my daughter not a daughter, at least in part, until their first heart noises registered in my ear—an identity formation that wasn't even possible when my grandfather was born in 1906 or when my father was born in 1945, and still only a rough science when I was born in 1971. But I know that, in many ways, I did not identify myself as a father until I heard my child's heartbeat, and that I couldn't have heard this before the discovery of the stethoscope. Most of us identify a doctor with the stethoscope, the intimate disc; but it is also parent and child identities twined together in that examination room, hopelessly dependent on the curl and twisting turns of simple listening technology, the only tool for the vital job of reading and feeling the rhythmic thumps of heart-noise, that signal of life we cannot see or otherwise sense.

In 2002 nine coal miners are trapped in the Quecreek Mine in Pennsylvania by rising water released after a drilling machine punches through a wall into an underground spring. The nine men—a father and son among the crew—retreat to the highest spot in the mine and rope themselves together. They listen for the signal from the surface—three small explosions—but don't hear anything. They start pounding on the roof bolts with their hammers, hoping to make some noise the surface can recognize. They pound and pound but background noise on the surface interferes and the seismic listening devices can't hear them. The men write notes to family members, seal them in a metal lunch box, and they wait to die. As rescuers work frantically to pull water from the mine with massive diesel powered pumps, they also drill down from the surface to pump oxygen into the cave where rescuers hope the men have retreated. If the miners are alive, they can only be in one place, all of them protected by a small womb of air against the rising flood. The miners continue pounding on the roof bolts, but they get no response. The miners' families gather on the surface, huddled in a tent around the drill operator. He is more than operator, more than muscle, and something like the human side of the machine. The listening side. The man with the touch. Watching the spin of metal. Waiting. When the drill finally reaches the lightless room, two hundred forty feet down, and punches like an amnio-needle into the pocket, the drill operator shuts off the machine, quiets the crowd, and he listens. I wonder what it was that he heard. How faint? How rhythmic? Perhaps a measured patient tapping. Perhaps a slam of metal to metal so urgent he felt it tingling from his own toes all the way up his spine. He listens, his hands on the machine, and finally hears or feels the rhythmic noise of the trapped men hammering at the steel—the sole musical evidence of survival. Above them, on the outside, the expectant wives and mothers rejoice. They hug the man at the drill and slap each other on the back—they can't wait to see and touch and smell their babies again.

ULTRASONIC

Lightning: This noise--the sharp *pop* and *twang* of a blue rubber ball as it rockets off simulated cat-gut strings, the resonant *crack* of it against the laminate wall; the different sort of *pop* and *pong* of it smacking off the back glass; the high-pitched *slap* of a well-hit shot, or a volley going off like firecrackers in a coat closet. Listen to a game of racquetball, eyes closed; you can hear the kill shots, hit low to the floor, and the long, looping shots that strike high and pinball around the upper walls. You can hear the *squeak, squeak* of shoes on the hardwood, the *slap and squeak* of soles, the *grunts* and *barks*, the *crashes* against the wall as players scramble around in the hard cage. Though I hadn't set foot on a court in years, I started playing racquetball again out of necessity in 2007. I craved the game and needed its release, now that there was a chance that the baby was in danger. I needed the loud sensory rush and the therapeutic noise. I appreciated the violent *smash* and *slam* of a simple blue orb and the way it allowed me to forget the tangible and the physical, that odd mark of a genetic screen. It's addictive. This leaving. When it was good, the boxed-in court took all the noise of my life and echoed it back, sending sound chasing the ball around and around like thunder chasing lightning, and shattered something in the rush.

Bump: The American Speech-Language-Hearing Association does not specifically record the noise of a racquetball court, but based on the chart of everyday noise levels they have recorded, the noise inside an enclosed court like the one I played on probably falls in the "painful" range of 120 to 150 decibels, similar to the noise from firearms, air raid sirens, jackhammers, or a jet plane take-off. It's possible that it's only in the "extremely loud" range along with rock music, model airplanes, bass drumrolls, chain saws and pneumatic drills. Either way, it seems clear that a single game of racquetball played without ear protection can irrevocably damage your hearing. ASLH mentions that excessive noise can also increase your blood pressure, upset your stomach, and cause insomnia. But another one of the side effects of damaging noise—say from an especially loud, bass bumping car stereo, or from a particularly heated racquetball game—is a kind of giddiness or euphoria. As they say, it can also "intensify the effects of drugs, alcohol, and aging." Noise can make you feel high; and like just about anything that gets you high, it can also harm your unborn baby. A baby's ears develop before her eyes. She knows your sound before she knows you through any other sense. She knows your noise before your silence.

Hissing: Definition alone says: *discordant, unwanted, unwelcome, lacking in agreeable musical quality, harsh, undesired, interfering, evil or slanderous report,* and by way of example *a hissing sound in a telephone receiver, static in a radio receiver, snow in a television receiver, forms of _____, the din or loud persistent incoherent sound that is a feature of most communities.* But what if the receiver appreciated the transcendent possibilities of snow? What if our family seemed to channel incoherence, seemed to feed on crisis?

Drum: In El Parque del Buen Retiro in Madrid, Spain, the hot summer Sundays of 2007 were given over to a kind of carnival atmosphere. Normally a busy but quiet place to visit, the park transformed on Sundays into a sea of people, and many of them were engaged in a sort of spiritual worship, a kind of transcendence through noise.

Families with children spread picnic blankets out, and groups of men passed soccer balls around. Young people sat in small groups, laughing, playing music, drinking and smoking. Sunbathers showed their skin, and paddleboats filled the lake. Children fed bread to the drum fish and carp. Venders circulated with ice cream, candy, toys; others set up shop to hawk T-shirts or tarot-card readings. Every Sunday night a graffiti-covered amphitheater filled with children who came for the regularly scheduled puppet shows.

El Parque del Buen Retiro sounded like something different—a din of voices and street musicians, whole bands of South American troubadours and the occasional lone bluesman playing his saxophone or his trumpet in the Metro stairwells because the acoustics there make him sound good. You might've heard a Korean man with a Casio keyboard singing Stevie Wonder songs. You might've heard a lot of strange things. But most of all what you heard, as soon as you set foot in the park, was the rolling rhythmic noise of drums. It was a kind of percussive background to everything else, a rumbling static snow that rose up from the memorial statue and rotunda, spilling across the lake.

If you got close to the noise, if you chased it across the park and stepped inside the marble rotunda, you found your senses bombarded by the overlapping and competing beats of drum circles. On any given Sunday there were ten or more groups of people sitting around or standing in circles, beating away on their drums, each group hitting their own marks; but also competing with or drowning out the surrounding circles. It was cacophonous and confusing, noise energy—a messy sort of noise that couldn't be contained—like the sound equivalent of an amusement park bumper-car ride where the plastic shells slam against each other beneath an electrified net.

You could see the sound's effect, though, in some of the participants and intimate audience members—the people who got close enough to the noise. You saw the way their eyes fluttered closed and their body seemed to move independently, their head sometimes flopping around as if it is barely attached, limbs loose as jelly.

The dancers and the drummers entered into a sort of trance-like state, a euphoric and giddy physical experience. If they were already high, the drum noise made them feel higher. And if they were sober, it gave them the giddy, heart-racing rush of drink and drug. It got them off. You could see it. Their faces appeared postcoital, flushed, and undeniably peaceful. For a few moments, they transcended this physical world.

To an outsider visiting in the summer of 2007, a man with a boy-child and a pregnant wife, it all sounded messy and indulgent, possibly dangerous and incoherent. To a man thinking about his unborn child—about tests, and trials, about telephone calls on a computer—the cops in stiff blue and Day-Glo vests appeared suddenly, perched at the edge of the rotunda on the cusp of violence. They seemed like they wanted to *bash* some skulls, *crack* some melons open on the marble steps. I could just about see it happening, could almost hear the dull *slap* of billy clubs on ribs and heads, the *crash* of drums hitting the pavement. The blue cops—the harsh physical reality of them as matter and energy—shattering the circles of noise, chasing the vibrations out of the rotunda, scattering the musicians out amongst the trees, drowning their sound out in the paddleboat-filled retention pond, shaking carp and drum and sunfish to the surface. Ever since the test results, I'd been lost in my own head. I was just waiting for something unbelievable to happen every day. Something to shake me back to the now. The park. The belly. The future. The boy clutching my hand in his own, pointing with the other at the silly man dancing. And the sound of the boy's laughter ringing off the marble.

Scream: The memory rush is part of the love too, part of the transcendence in racquetball. Proust had his cookie. For me the racquetball court has its sensory triggers. The smell of sweat baked into the hardwood floor and the Masonite walls. The almost claustrophobic, cell-like feeling. The white paint streaked with blue marks, black streaks, and round dirty dots—the ball-scuffs and racquet-tags of heated competition. Even the chemical glare of fluorescent lights can take me back. But the naked, angry, violent sound of it sends me sifting through memories and thinking about the color of noise.

I remember my father and the Judge rattling the walls. These leading citizens: Fathers. Husbands. Grown men exposed in shorts and sweatbands. Rec-Specs and big fat white wristbands. The Judge wore knee pads. Sometimes Dad came home with big purple bruises that turned black and yellow and blue—as if the ball had left some of its rubber on his flesh.

Dad never missed his racquetball games; even after the divorce when it was harder for him to escape, harder to leave us kids with Mom. He just took us along for the show and the sport of it.

On the court, my father and the Judge transformed. They became different people. Or they let go of themselves. I'd watch them beforehand in the locker room smiling, laughing, telling stories and acting like the best of friends—talking the small talk of business, family, sports and weather. But when they stepped on the court, something changed. They became fiercely competitive, loud and aggressive, potentially violent. They were swaggering assholes who barked at each other, cursed mistakes, and argued bitterly over calls.

"In!" one of them would yell.

"Oh, bullshit!" the other would bark.

"FUCK!"

"SON-OF-A-BITCH!"

And back and forth they'd volley.

I was always enraptured by the way their noise echoed and reverberated, rising up over the walls of the courts and filling my ears with *fuck, goddamn, shit, motherfucker, bullshit, Jesus H. Christ*, and all the other glorious blue language of competition. The whole place resonated with their unrestrained noise; and still today when I step onto the racquetball court and try to forget the present reality, I can summon the racquet club courts of my past, the smells, and the sound of my own father in full bloom.

Womb: Perhaps there are times when we must embrace discordance and incoherence, when we don't need musical quality. Perhaps one of those times is when we are sleeping babies, or when we are thinking about sleeping babies.

For our needs, there's the Obus Forme Sound Therapy white-noise machine, the Sound Oasis Sound Therapy machine, the Sleep Mate 980, the Sound Conditioner, the Hometics SoundSpa Relaxation Machine, the SoundScreen 580 and 980, the LifeSounds 440, and many many others; and these machines produce repetitive sound "tapestries" with names like Surf, Country Eve, White Sound, Thunderstorm, and Brook all in an effort to help you fall asleep faster and sleep through the night. Many of these noise machines are marketed to parents of babies or small children, suggesting that they will help your child have more relaxing healthier sleep, which is good for brain development. This is what they say.

Some of them suggest that the white noise emanating from the machine will mimic the sounds of the womb—implying that your forthcoming baby number two or even the boy might be happier and more comfortable back inside. Almost all of them include the words "therapy" or "spa" in their title or description, but they are often marketed as "white noise" machines—all of it suggesting that noise, at least some levels of it, may actually have therapeutic value. Noise is medicine. Noise is a drug. They want to hook you early, just out of the womb.

Once when I was in graduate school, my girlfriend and I stayed with the children of a family friend while the parents went on an anniversary vacation; and we soon discovered that all of them were hooked on noise. Each bedroom in the house was equipped with at least one white-noise machine and the entire family—especially the children—was completely dependent on

31

them for sleep. Without their machines, I was led to believe that the children would roam the house like zombies, eternally awake and terrified of the silence.

I've known many people who can't ease their mind and relax enough to achieve a restful and rejuvenating sleep state without the drone of a fan or the din of a television or radio in the background. For many people noise is relaxing and comforting, safe and peaceful. It is an escape. For some, they can't sleep without noise; and by extension—since sleep is necessary for overall health and survival—they can't live without some kind of noise, some kind of escape from the monotonous pummel of waiting.

Move: With our first-born son, it was Eminem in utero. It was P. Diddy, Biggie Smalls, Dr. Dre and Snoop Dogg bumping in the womb. During her second pregnancy, my wife became obsessed with the more recent crop of bass thumping, party music, 50-Cent, Jay-Z, Justin Timberlake, Rihanna, and so forth. All hip-hop, R & B, and rap; all bass heavy and loud, all of it sexually suggestive. She couldn't really explain it. There's something about pregnancy, she said, that made her love it. It made her happy.

The music transformed her into a teenager singing along in the car. The song had to have a driving beat and a catchy chorus. It had to make you want to move. That's all that mattered. She knew many of the lyrics were sexist and inane; and she found it just as darkly comic as I did that our 5-year-old son could sing an R & B melody that included the lines, "Hey sexy lady, it was nice to know ya. Now I gotta move on."

At some point, she knew, like I did, that the baby inside was listening too. Hearing develops early and the parenting books all say that the baby begins to recognize your voice while still in the womb. They even suggest that you read aloud to your fetus and play music. Some books warn against loud music or excessive noise and the damage it can cause in utero. Maybe this blue noise on the radio was bad noise. But it made my wife feel good.

Nothing was going to stop her from listening to her rump-shaking rhythm tracks. Nothing was going to stop her from bouncing to her noise. The music made her feel good at a time when feeling good couldn't be taken for granted. They helped transcend the physical. And it was sort of funny to watch her shake her swollen belly and lip sync to the radio—even if I could barely stand to listen. It all sounded like repetitive noise to me, inane nonsense that was about as compelling as static snow on the TV.

As soon as the baby was out, she didn't give up hip-hop for

good, but her passion for it waned. Whatever it was about the music that made her feel good during her first pregnancy got flushed out with the amniotic fluid. I often wondered what it sounded like inside her. I wondered if the bass beats rippled through womb; and I wondered if the baby would roll and shudder and shake to the beat before it walked. I wondered if it would walk at all on the outside or ever run fast enough to get away from our mistakes.

Thud: During periods of prolonged physical exertion or stress, the brain releases endorphins, or naturally produced opiates, into the body, causing feelings of euphoria, elation, and even invincibility. This "runner's high" has often been compared to an orgasm; and this may explain why so many people get addicted to distance running.

Yiannis Kouros, extreme distance runner, described what he feels when he runs.

> At that time I feel that I stay outside of my body. It is as if I see my body in front of me; my mind commands and my body follows. This is a very special feeling, which I like very much. . . It is a very beautiful feeling and the only time I experience my personality separate from my body, as two different things.[3]

Other athletes have reported such orgasmic transcendence of the physical as well; but it is most often reported after extended or prolonged activity. It is often a product of almost masochistic, abusive movement, a pounding of the body into submission; and, I suspect, also a product of the rhythm and sound of sport. Many who have experienced the so-called "runner's high" also report heightened sensory awareness, a kind of *a priori* knowledge that enables greater physical coordination and an ability to see and hear better.

For some athletes, the rush of endorphins does not produce *very special and very beautiful feelings* but a physical and emotional shrinking, a kind of sensory overload and depression of awareness. This echoes my experience with running. I don't enjoy running much—unless it's in short bursts between two basketball goals or within the walls of a racquetball court. There's nothing remotely orgasmic about running for me. Perhaps it's my flat feet or my

---

3   Yiannis Kouros, "A War Is Going On Between My Body and My Mind," *Ultrarunning*, March 1990, p. 19.

bad knees. But I don't feel high when I run. I feel stupid, slow, and clumsy. All I hear is my labored breathing, my feet thudding on the sidewalk, and my heartbeat *swish, swishing* in my ears.

If jogging is like sex then every time I jog is like my first fuck—awkward, painful, and regrettable enough to make me curl up in bed afterward and wish it had never happened.

The only exception is on the racquetball court.

On the court my running is confined to a small space, a rectangle, a clearly marked boundary. Walls. Glass walls that contain the ball, keeping it close, tight and in my same orbit, the two of us floating around together in the liquid space of sound. My running here is part of play, part of the game. The point is not the running but the effect.

Fluid: In Madrid, Spain, just blocks from the Sunday noise and bustle of El Parque del Buen Retiro, tucked behind the Museo Arqueológico Nacional, sat the Hotel Recoletos, a dark, hard-edged hotel without a visible sign--no indication that it was, in fact, a "hotel." This should have been our first clue.

In the summer of 2007 a few random French and German tourists, visiting teachers like me, my pregnant wife, and our 5-year-old son populated the Recoletos--but most brazenly Spanish businessmen and their high-dollar prostitutes used the hotel for their business.

It had a different sort of atmosphere. Not what you would necessarily call "family friendly." It wasn't Disneyland, but we loved it. Or at least I did.

The place was totally inappropriate. Noisy and blue. But it had character. It had people to watch—people like Toni the snaggle-toothed maid who liked to arrange our son's stuffed animals on his bed and who talked so fast I never had any idea what she was saying. And then there were the whores . . . these weren't the transvestite whores or the African or Asian hookers you'd find on different streets in Madrid. These were young white girls, many of them Eastern European, their thick perfume competing in the hotel bar with the ever-present cloud of cigarette smoke and leaving pungent floral trails in the tiny Recoletos elevators. They all had a very severe sort of beauty—one colored and smudged by their jobs, their old johns, and this hotel.

The boys at the counter—most of them brothers from the same family—all worked as de facto pimps and the bartender, affectionately called El Duro, provided a surly, but still somehow comforting, wake-up call for me in the mornings. Three days a week for almost a month I ordered a *caffè Americano* and a croissant, and I sat there and scribbled down comments on student writing, trying not to think about blood tests or how a fetus can fail one.

There at the Recoletos, with the 80s mix music, the cigarette smoke, and the Spanish words drifting over my head, they had no concerns for ultrasound or amniocentesis, no concern for what it's like talking through a computer to a nurse in California named Veronica about triple screens and quad screens, about alpha fetal protein. El Duro barely spoke to me. He didn't like me. He didn't care if I didn't like him. He didn't care or understand how a voice trickling from your computer speaker resonates so many miles away or how one little score on one test out of four can shake you and nearly put you on the next flight home. El Duro didn't know how a fetus fails a test either or how the only answers may come from what we can extract from the amniotic fluid or what we see by sending sound waves bouncing through the womb.

Twinkle: The morning after we talked to the nurse again, through a computer in a hotel room, we stood on the Eiffel Tower deck. We watched fighter jets thunder overhead, streaking the sky with red, white, and blue smoke. Bastille Day in Paris. We were enveloped in the noise of celebration. And still we had no answers. I wanted to curse someone, but it wouldn't do any good—my voice drowned out in the wash of distance and direction. Later, we witnessed paratroopers drop from a helicopter, bloom and drift down like twirling seeds into a park nearby; and I would think of our endangered baby. That night we gathered on the pedestrian bridge over the River Seine with crackers and cheese and cans of beer and our healthy boy, and we held him tight, clutched to our chests, our noses buried in his hair, and listened to the boom-boom of the fireworks and the din of drunken crowds, and we watched with hope as the Tower blossomed and twinkled with a million white lights. There was no other way to look at it.

Wish: If you want it to, a fetal heartbeat in utero sounds something like *wish, wish, wish, wish*. And three weeks later when the doctor back home moved the wand around my wife's belly and pointed at the sound-picture on the monitor, we could see the little heart thumping and pumping for us. We could see the *wish, wish, wish*—the rhythm first—and it was undeniably therapeutic. That sound tapestry. That white noise. We were there for the ultrasound and the amniocentesis. We were there for answers. But it wouldn't come that day. No sound beyond that image. But that image gave us so much peace.

For three weeks already we'd waited, hidden away in the Hotel Recoletos in Madrid, taking trips to Retiro Park for the puppet shows and the playgrounds and the noise. Not knowing. Wondering. What does it all mean? What will we do if . . . ? Now we were home. And we were afraid.

The doctor moved the wand over my wife's belly. "The baby is moving around a lot," he said, and the sound image dissolved into shades of gray, shadows, and strange fragments. He stopped, clicked a button, and snapped a picture.

I wanted to ask him what the baby hears when the sound waves envelope its body, bouncing off and back to us. Does it feel good? Is it therapeutic white noise? Or is it something more discordant, unwanted, and unwelcome chasing her around? Is it white or blue or some other color? I wanted to ask. But I didn't.

In holistic healing practice, yoga, and other spiritual disciplines, the blue or fifth chakra, is located in the throat and typically associated with self-expression, honesty, and decision-making. Physical dysfunctions due to a sick blue chakra are things such as laryngitis, lockjaw, or other mouth and throat problems that make it difficult to speak. If you are expressing yourself honestly, openly, releasing all your pent-up emotion and anger, then a divine blue energy flows through your fifth chakra.

You go blue.

In the end, they punctured my wife's belly with a long heavy-gauge needle. I sat in chair in the corner, quietly watching the sound picture on the computer screen. We saw the baby reach instinctively for the needle and I wanted to scream, "No, don't!" But I didn't say a word. I didn't know if anyone would hear my voice. In the end, the only answer came from fluid flowing around us; and later, words trickled through a telephone receiver. Not static. Not snow. The peace of knowing one thing. Our baby was healthy. But it was still the sound of one question answered and many more asked. The sound of one hand clapping. The smack of a blue ball against a white wall.

Wash: Not long after the tests I went to play racquetball alone, without an opponent to muddle up my music. I settled into a rhythm, an individual volley of serve and return, and had the ball moving. Singing. Lighting fast. It was safer this way. Alone. I could feel the noise, feel the transcendence, and keep it contained in the court. *Pow, pow, pow.* I got high with only minimal hearing damage, potential euphoria, and possible confusion; but there was nothing the sound could do to our baby now—no therapy, no damage, no pictures it could paint that I couldn't face. The ball bounced of the walls and zinged through the air. I got up on my toes, bent my knees, and held the racquet in front. The game is all about angles and patience. You have to feel the flow and find a way to zero in on that bouncing blue ball. You have to understand patience and power. I followed-through on a forehand and the ball slammed hard against the front wall. I stutter-stepped back and returned it with a backhand, straight down the middle. Then I stepped into another forehand, following through across my body, and the ball returned fast. I shuffled back and powered into another return. Soon the sound was *wham, wham, wham, wham.* It was good. And when it was really good, the noise washed over me, the ball seemed to slow down, dragging through the air—I could see two bounces ahead and know where it would fall. Time stalled and crept, bent to the rhythm of the game, the noise of the moment. I was enveloped. Swathed in sound. It was a kind of out-of-body experience, a transcendence enabled by the noise. Elevated. Aloft. Drifting, floating above. I left the court flushed and spent, exhausted but elated; and it was not over, but it was good enough for the moment, good enough to get me through until tomorrow. The baby would be there soon. The baby. Just months away now. And I heard her coming. I heard she would be blue at first, screaming, then perfectly pink.

ALL OF A DITHER

"Look out!' squawked Mrs. Mallard, all of a dither. 'You'll get run over!'"
—*Make Way for Ducklings,* by Robert McCloskey

An etymology of*: The dithering of grass,* says a resurrected Wallace Stevens, while *the stage manager was dithering in the wings. Faced with unpleasant choices, she merely dithers. She dithers on the phone,* at the coffee pot, the water-cooler, over donuts at Church; but perhaps now is the perfect time for confusion and agitation, even while *wild rumors of war dithered the population.* Truthfully *the outbreak of war threw all parties into a dither.* And here in the everyday theater, something had to be done about our birth writer, the navigator and guide through this essay. Before the baby arrived he seemed stuck in some kind of amniotic rut, a comfortable groove, a track of language and origins. He thought he had things all figured out, thought his life, perhaps too predictably, ran like a machine, all the gauges reading normal, and he wondered why they needed another child, wondered what it would prove or add to their existence. But in his head now, with the baby coming, the newly resurrected Mr. Stevens kept repeating, "*The dithering of grass. The dithering of grass. The dithering of grass,*" until the navigator, shaken out of his own nervous tizzy, dropped the curtain and Stevens, rising unsteadily from his stool, wobbled forward and teetered around on stage, moved it seems by words and mumbled stage directions. Our navigator, lost in the lights, could only vacillate between choices, essaying in his head down one path or the other, dithering on the page until the applause subsided and poor Wallace Stevens keeled forward into the orchestra pit, exhausting his potential, an error of narration that frightened the audience into a rolling tizzy, a trembling wave of panic that sent them scrambling, the energy of the audience's fear and confusion multiplying and expanding until the gold-crusted room was engorged with emotion and people pressed against the exits, stepping over some and on top of others, bursting through the doors, out into the rain-wet streets quivering with bodies; and everywhere was the trembling bandy-legged noise of new-birth, escape and raw salvation.[4]

---

4   Italicized passages taken from "Dither," Philip Babcock Gove, ed. *Webster's Third New International Dictionary of the English Language* (Merriam-Webster, 2002).

First knowledge of: Before our children become the doughy, loose-limbed, soft-skulled and tangible things we can touch and hold and smell—that sweet milky odor, the cheesy stink of their skin folds, and the powdery scent of their heads. Before my daughter made a noise, I knew her body by pictures painted through sound, pictures that looked reptilian and warped, bones glowing white beneath transparent flesh. It was difficult to feel like a father from those pictures. Before she walked, I could know the ripple and flutter of her kicks. But before she made a noise, her first voice was the *wish-wish-wish* of her heartbeat filtered through an electronic stethoscope. Before she saw me make words, she knew the sound of my voice, the rumble of my baritone, the rattle of my cough, even the low growl of my snores at night. Before perhaps she'd even developed ears, she resonated sound in her bones and tissue, her whole body trembling like a tuning fork to the everyday noise of our lives—the howling passing of trains, the white noise of the I-80 and I-41 freeways, barking dogs, the nightly oscillating drone of the police helicopters, and on better nights the soft sounds of my voice reading to her mother's belly, talking into the button, my voice vibrating through the amniotic drum. With each child, I knew so little that I wondered how I would register the arrival, how each child would rattle my gauges.

A history of: *Airplane bombers used mechanical computers to perform navigation and bomb trajectory calculations. Curiously, these computers (boxes filled with hundreds of gears and cogs) performed more accurately when the aircraft was in flight, and less well on when the airplane was on the ground. Engineers realized that the vibration from the aircraft reduced the error from sticky moving parts. Instead of moving in short jerks, they moved more continuously. Small vibrating motors were built into the computers, and their vibration was called dither from the Middle English verb "didderen," meaning, "to tremble." Today, when you tap a mechanical meter to increase its accuracy, you are applying dither.*[5]

My father's explanation for the effect of childbirth on my life: "It'll reset all your meters."

I don't know if he means the act or the effect, the fact or the love that pins the needle into the red zone.

5   Ken Pohlmann, *Principles of Digital Audio* (McGraw-Hill, 5th Edition, 2005).

A trope of: *Otherwise known as "Ape Mechanics," or a "Fonzarelli Fix"... In real life, it works best (when it works at all) when dealing with machines with moving parts capable of being physically jammed or temporarily impeded (gears or switches), hydraulic systems suffering particular kinds of plugs or clogs (fuel lines or sump pumps), or internal components whose function depends on precise alignment and which have become misaligned somehow (vacuum tubes, early transistors, and connection interfaces) ... all hallmarks of pulp storytelling when technology was still a hands-on art. Realistically, it is almost impossible to work with modern delicate electronics or futuristic solid-state circuitry/ machinery, but the appeal of a highly emotive and easy-to-show repair technique often wins out over boring technical accuracy.*[6]

Real-life dithers are disappearing with the rise of digital. Percussive maintenance has become as anachronistic as mix-tape references are to the CD and MP3 generation. We still whack the digital DVD player, shake an iPod, or smack the computer screen—perhaps because we want to deny that we cannot dither our way out of a problem, because we want to hope we have the power to make machines run better, that we can un-stick what is stuck—but mostly we are impotent without analog, dumbed by digital technology that only responds to language, not the rough physical fixes of our Ape Mechanics. But maybe dither is different. Maybe it's a storytelling trope because it represents a fundamental human need—to be reminded that we are not the victims of our own intelligence, that machines are not our masters. Maybe it also persists figuratively because we live in a rutted world at times, and it's easy to fall into one, easy to find yourself making the same mistakes over and over again, sitting in front of a television for an average of 6 hours a day. We need

---

6   "Percussive Maintenance," tvtropes.org, TV Tropes Foundation, LLC.

the occasional whack of percussive maintenance—reminding us what it means to be alive.

When I approached the neglected fish-tank in my son's room, I was often certain the blue Beta fish was dead. It wasn't until I tapped the glass that I saw any sign of life—the fish darting and zipping wildly around the tank before settling back again into it's corner. Is that what I'm circling around? Is this not dither, too? Perhaps for the fish. But dither is more significant in my pregnant student's Navy pilot-husband tapping his "standby attitude indicator'" on cold mornings before he disappears into the sky; and it's still there in the farmer who takes a screwdriver handle to the starter solenoid on his old Ford truck before he rattles off into the fields.

In the eternal dream of movies it's Whoopi Goldberg's fist to the computer in *Jumpin' Jack Flash*. Dither is magic over logic, sound over sense. It's mystery and madness. It's forever Fonzie's fist to the jukebox in Al's Diner, Chewbacca's punch to the Millennium Falcon's hyperdrive. It's the big-screen kiss, a kick to the shin, Marty McFly's head to the time-traveling DeLorean. It's the slap to the face of the hysterical character, the shake of the shoulders, and the *SNAP OUT OF IT* screamed. Despite its role as a pop-culture trope, a storytelling technique, whose real-life analogues are fewer and further between, we're still able to find dither, the Fonzarelli fix, in the cockpit of an F-18 Hornet—one of the most advanced flying machines ever engineered—on a cold-fog morning in Lemoore, California, or on a pitching deck in the middle of an ocean, in the hands of a man with a wife and baby at home, as he tap-tap-taps a finger to his indicator—the percussive sound of human intervention against the indifference of a machined world.

An accounting of: I have come to believe that dither is also the spiritual tremble. It's the physical and the mental, the ecstatic agitation of Kierkegaard before God, Thompson before Vegas, or believers before Jesus on Toast, on Tortilla, Grill Stain, Grilled Cheese, Lourdes, or Medjugorje. It is non-believers, too, the secular searchers prostrate before the sublime, quivering breathless before a painting or a sunset or a game-winning shot. It's what the grass does on a windy day, what children do on a playground. But it's also how an essay or book moves sometimes. Bouncing thoughts around. Vacillating between opposing ideas or intentions. And dither can be a metaphorical smack to the face, a fist-bump, bitch-slap to your rhythm—a ball peen hammer whacking your clogs loose, freeing up the flow and making the narrative machine work better or smarter somehow. In stories it's those moments of surprise or grace that O'Connor capitalized upon, the epiphanies of Joyce and the razor cuts of Carver and Didion, the blunt fierce sentences of Hempel or Hemingway. But here is what any storyteller must hope: that a true tremble, an honest dither, can be simple, subtle, or sensational. The feeling is what a sentence, an image can do to your head, or what the birth of a child does to your internal meters. Dithers are at work around us every day, if we tune our instruments into the right frequency, if we tap them before liftoff and let them guide us through the noise.

A definition of: *steven:* n: [ME, fr. OE stefn, stemn voice, OHG, stimna, stimma, Goth stibna] 1: VOICE 2: NOISE, UPROAR[7]

Until the 1980s, and longer in some places, it was common practice for the ob-gyn, upon delivering a baby into the world, to administer a hard slap to the back or bottom to get the baby to cry and thereby draw his first breath. The welcome slap, a dither of sorts, was ostensibly meant to help the baby's lungs kick into operation, and the baby's first warbling cry was a welcome sound, one that doctor's and parents waited to hear.

A silent baby was a troubling baby.

The story of my own birth goes like this: My mother punched the doctor for trying to give her drugs she didn't want. Then I was born, and I didn't make a sound. Later they brought my mother the wrong baby, a noisy crying baby.

She said, "That's not my baby."

"How do you know?"

"I just know. That's not my baby."

When they brought her the right baby, I just stared up at the room of blue scrubs like a fish, wide-eyed with wonder, and didn't make a sound.

There is no record of whether the doctor applied percussive maintenance to me, no story of a slap to the back, a smack to the rump, or a Fonzarelli fix to get me to cry and draw my first breath. There is only the image of my silence, my eyes staring up, "Like you were just taking it all in," Mom always said.

Recent studies have suggested that the percussive maintenance of the newborn slap is vastly overrated and, in fact, potentially

---

7   "Steven," Philip Babcock Gove, ed. *Webster's Third New International Dictionary of the English Language* (Merriam-Webster, 2002).

detrimental to the baby's ability to breathe normally. Research has shown that babies breathe just fine on their own and simply don't need the doctor's dither.

Other research and numerous books have also indicated that it's just not nice to smack a newborn baby. It hurts. Most babies don't like it. Not at all. Most of them cry and scream when you hit them. Some of them—the troubling ones--simply stare at the offending Doctor as if to say, "Don't. Do. That."

And all of them slap you back. Eventually. Every child shakes up the world.

First sound of: The story of my daughter's birth goes like this: First she was "a boy." Then she was an arm. And a head. Then she was a baby. Then she was a girl. "A baby girl!" the young doctor said finally, righting her stumbles as best she could before the nurse peeked around the drape and confirmed, "It's a girl." But in a sense the doctor was right about our baby. She was everything immediately. And while they don't smack babies any longer, they do stick their gloved fingers down their throat and wipe them roughly with a towel before handing the father the scissors and showing him where to make the symbolic cut, the cut only for ceremony after a cesarean birth. I carried her tiny body across the hall, through the double doors, past my smiling in-laws, into the nursery. The nurses took her from me and laid her down beneath what felt like a fast-food heat lamp as they wiped her down, weighed her, measured her and just generally messed with her. I noticed every other baby in the room sleeping or eating happily, silent as a picture. But not my girl of noise. I watched her body temperature rise in red digital numbers. She screamed and screamed, clutching her tiny trembling hands into tight fists, the veins in her face pulsing purple under the skin. She screamed when they pricked her heel for blood tests, and she screamed when they pressed her inky foot against the paper. She screamed long and loud for at least a half an hour until they let me hold her close, tucked up against my blue scrubs, and carry her back to her waiting mother.

The effect of: In modern sound engineering, *dither* is an intentionally applied form of noise used to randomize error. It keeps mistakes from becoming permanent patterns—like a small fire to keep away the larger ones, a wake-up call. For optimal sound, you want generalized agitation + a localized jolt from time to time. Blue noise makes a good dither. It helps to clean up the speckles of noise, the small errors in translation between analog and digital that can become systemic, widespread, and sound like a whisper or hiss under the mix. When you apply dither with blue noise, it nudges an error out of its rut, unsticks an audio clog, and scatters the impact of unwanted mess. It keeps you from getting stuck in the past or in the in betweens, keeps your sound true and not too perfect. It keeps the resurrected Wallace Stevens wobbling between the audience and the director, suspended there in eternal vacillation.

The birth of: Some of us have dithers forced upon us. They fall into our laps as we're sitting there, trying to follow the story. We change jobs, lose jobs, lose friends. Some of us make our own dithers and set ourselves atremble for a lifetime. We make babies. We conceive small motors, little engines of blue noise and chaos, to keep the machines agitated, to keep our hearts honest and strong and humming through the air of days. A child drops into your life and you never stop moving, never take the sound of meters for granted, and time slips past small windows like wispy cirrus clouds, barely noticed as you buzz low across the checkerboard landscape of years, staring down at the pockets of blue water amidst the ancient furrowed sea bottom—the whine of your jets droning white under all that sky.

SEVEN FATHOMS DOWN

1 FATHOM/6'

If an experience was to literally *warm the cockles of your heart* it would have to heat up the valves between the aortal chambers. Even a cold heart has cockles because a cockle is a simple valve and muscle; but a cockle is also mussel and sound, sea creature and white noise, object and metaphor. It is a word with physicality, with body and breath, surface and depth. Perhaps what we mean when we use such clichés is that the warming of one's cockles enables the heart valves to work smoothly, effortlessly, and efficiently; or perhaps when a cockle is warmed it dilates open wide and blood flushes fast through the opening, the heart fills with blood and swells. What you're saying is, "My heart is flooded."

The dictionary tells me that, figuratively speaking, "cockles," in this context, refers to one's innermost feelings and emotions, and the phrase does seem to suggest an intense flush or flood of feeling; and though the operation of our heart valves is mostly an unconscious involuntary body function, the heart muscle also responds to emotion and to the unconscious signals of stress or love or fear or excitement sent from our brains. The faster our heart pumps the warmer our cockles become.

A *cockle* is also a bivalve mussel, a shellfish with a heart-shaped shell. And *to cockle* means to pucker or gather into folds. When you give someone a kiss, you *cockle* your lips. When your baby daughter reaches out her tiny hand and gathers up your shirt in her fist, she's *cockling* the fabric. And when a wave breaks on a beach you hear it *cockling* on the sand like a whisper.

Cockle is object, animal, metaphor and sound. And when a turn of phrase or a line of language tries to warm the cockles of a reader, chances are those words are flirting with nostalgia, that unique sickness of memory that's defined as a sentimental longing for the past.

Occasionally as a boy I would stumble across a conch shell, maybe at a friend's house, sequestered on a shelf of knickknacks, and I'd be tempted to touch it, to hold it up to my head. Pink and white, it looked almost human, like an enormous calcified ear. But it was an ear with a voice. I'd press the shell to my own ear, listening to its hushed secrets. We lived in Kansas, and I'd only seen the ocean once or twice in my life. Most of our family vacations took us to the mountains of Colorado, and summers were spent playing in cold-water streams, building dams of river rock. Today I'm mildly afraid of the ocean, convinced that it wants to hurt me, that it wishes me ill and dislikes my body's intrusion into its body. My son, born in Colorado, but identifying as a Californian in most ways, charges into the waves unafraid, letting them bash him about. To him the ocean doesn't seem malevolent. He seems to have long shed my baggage of fear, and it does crank and flush the valves of my heart to see him happy. Such moments with my children stretch the intimate muscle until it pumps so full I think it might break some ribs. It's almost enough to recapture the romantic relationship I had with the ocean as a landlocked child who grew up on muddy lakes and loved the magic of placing an ear to the conch shell, hearing the faint white noise of an ocean's waves cockling against a distant shore.

2 FATHOMS/12'

Sound and sight will always be intimately, synesthetically connected, if only through the metaphors we choose, the language we employ feebly conveying our effort to see and understand through sound. But sound is more than metaphor and form. Sound has body and weight. Sound is practical. It's a tool and a lens. We see with sound when we are functionally blind or when light cannot penetrate the place we're looking, when we need to see in the dark or beneath the surface of something vast and impenetrable. We use sound to see under skin, bone, muscle, and tissue, beneath the earth's crust on the surface of the planet, or to extend our vision deep into a body of water. We use sound to map mine-tunnels and the terrain of the ocean floor. We use sound to find signs of life or death from trapped miners; we use it to explore caverns and cavities, and to discover tumors or capture earthquake tremors. We witness through sound what we can't see through the eyes. Sound can now give us a three-dimensional digital image of our growing baby, a picture of the future conjured up on a computer monitor; and sound can show a fish or school of fish swimming in the water. Sound can help the fisherman find his catch. And sometimes I sound my way through an essay, navigating by means of echolocation—flying blind in the dark, sending out a signal of sorts, listening to what bounces back.

3 FATHOMS/18'

Consider the catfish. Bottom feeders. Freshwater shit-filters. They only come to the surface occasionally, to roll in the shallows, exposing their white bellies. I've been thinking about catfish lately, perhaps because I spent much of my teenage years around these odd creatures and I sometimes credit fishing with saving me from the kind of trouble that found a lot of my classmates in high school. When they were partying, I was often fishing.

My best friend and I regularly skipped the big house parties and the keggers in the country so we could sit up all night fishing for channel catfish at a lake outside of town. We used spin-cast fishing rods and chicken livers for bait. And as much as I liked fishing for them, I didn't particularly enjoy catching them. I didn't like handling catfish. They seemed prehistoric and wicked, and if you didn't hold them just right, gripping them hard with your fingers behind their front fins, they'd thrash around and spine you. My friend, on the other hand, would hold them up to his face and "talk" to them. Catfish make a kind of croaking sound like a frog and he would croak back at them before pulling the treble hook out with pliers and tossing them back.

Noodling is fishing for catfish with your hands. In the Kaw River it means swimming blind in the muddy waters, diving down, feeling along the bottom for sink-holes or trees under which a catfish might be resting, using your hands to see the bottom feeders. My father did this a couple of times in college. The big ones, often channel cats or flatheads, park themselves on the bottom facing into the current and they don't move. They use their negative buoyancy and their heavy bony skulls to settle into the mud and let the current push food past their wide toothless mouths.

Much like a shark, a catfish's whole body is covered with sensory receptors that allow it to smell and taste anything that touches it or passes by it in the water. Catfish don't have scales. They have skin. They also use their namesake cat-like barbels, or "whiskers" to reach out into the muck and navigate, feeling and smelling for a passing meal. If you're dragging a chicken liver past them and they should happen to sense the bait, they will strike quick and hard; and if you're not careful, they'll take your line and drag it deeper. They'll find a log and tangle you up until your line breaks and your fish story becomes a fight story.

If you're noodling, however, you have to get down to their level, down to the bottom, surprise a fish and grab it with both hands in front of its spiny poisonous fins, or you have to cram your hand down its toothless mouth and drag it up to the surface. A catfish's bony fins are barbed and can emit a stinging protein strong enough in some breeds to disable or kill a human. The Kansas channel cats I encountered just made you bleed and ache for a day or so, sort of like a bee sting. But legend holds that in the old days, the catfish, particularly the river cats, were bigger and meaner. Fishermen used to pull giant catfish out of the Kaw, some as big as 200 pounds—a fish that must have been absolutely terrifying and prehistoric-looking; and I've heard stories of 500-pound catfish in the Mississippi River. I've seen a 50 pounder in a tank at a bait shop and it was grotesquely huge, its skin mottled white, purple, and black, like a corpse. It looked like something out of a horror film—dumb, wet, and malevolent.

The old noodlers used a hay hook to land the big ones and stories tell of the frustrated fisherman who, after losing one too many, tied his hook to his wrist with a stout hemp rope. The foolhardy fisherman went into the Kaw, determined to land a big cat, to pull something big up to the surface, and he was never seen again—dragged to the bottom and drowned by his subject, the two of them tied together forever.

Radar uses sound waves to see, and if an entity or idea "flies under your radar," it operates outside of the line of sight, even beyond of reach of the sound waves. More figuratively, it exists outside of the focus or immediate area of attention. Radar acts and moves unnoticed, practically invisible. Such stealthy ideas or memories or experiences may very well influence your thinking in ways that are unseen and difficult to articulate. I believe most of us are fishing for ghosts—those spectral ideas about life and death that hover at the edge of our consciousness or just beneath the surface of our waking life. Sight promises knowledge; but perhaps it's only by closing our eyes and listening, by echo-navigating through the landscape of memory that we can explore the unseen terrain below. Sound is used to "see" during warfare because we understand that the most meaningful adversary, the most insidious vehicle of espionage is often the vessel operating beneath the radar, moving fast and low to the ground, just outside the peripheral vision, or traveling below the surface of the water. These are the vehicles that can bring you down before you realize what has hit you.

The word "fathom" refers to both the unit of measurement and to the practice of measuring the depth of a body of water by means of "sounding" lines. But the practice is also called a "sounding," or "taking a sounding." Here's how it works: one sailor, known as the leadsman is charged with one of the most important jobs on the ship—to see, or rather *feel* the unseen terrain beneath the water's surface. To "fathom" means that the sailor drops a lead-weighted sounding line over the side. The rope spools through his coarse hands and the leadsman waits for it to hit bottom and go slack; then he might let it bounce and drag a bit over the bottom before hauling it in, feeling the changing tensions in the rope. When ready to measure depth, the leadsman grabs the line loosely with one hand and pulls it through with the other, stretching his arms out as far as they can reach, quickly pinching and counting off each time, hollering the number of fathoms up to the captain or first mate. A fathom is roughly six feet, the same depth at which you bury a man.

A good captain, with the help of his leadsman, can discern the depth of the water and, therefore, know how far he was from land or if they were traveling through dangerous waters. A good leadsman is like an oracle seeing in the dark. A good leadsman can guide the boat past unseen obstacles lurking beneath the surface, sandbars or rocks that can rip a hole in his hull or ground the ship. To fathom then is to measure the depth of a body of water, but fathom is also the unit of measurement. It is action and form, verb and noun, sounding and seeing through careful touch.

The more scientifically inclined leadsman might fathom with a weighted basket of sorts and a hunk of sticky tallow, by which he takes sediment samples from the ocean floor, using them to help determine the ship's geographical location. To fathom is not just navigation but also an effort to understand the unseen ocean terrain in a way that other sailors cannot touch. The lines are an extension of the leadsman's own limbs, a long arm or a tentacle; but they've mostly been replaced in modern times by sonar technology, or echo sounding, a process that uses a transponder to generate sound waves and bounce them off the ocean floor, and then translates them into a reproduction of the topography on a computer monitor. Today's sailors mostly measure with waves instead of lines.

Ultrasound machines and fish-finders work in similar ways. The human element is mostly removed from mapping the unseen, or at least reduced to reading output on a screen. Of course it's a more complete picture of hidden terrain, all the canyons and crevasses, the mountains and valleys of the ocean floor, a more comprehensive picture of the dangers below.

Just as the digital heart monitor has largely replaced the stethoscope as the primary tool of auscultation for cardiologists and obstetricians, for sailors the traditional sounding line has been replaced by echo sounding technology. Though I might argue here that the leadsman with his plummet and doctor with his stethoscope are able to see through sound in ways that a computer can never truly approximate, the picture provided is admittedly a less accurate, less comprehensive map, shaped as much by not-knowing, by uncertainty and mystery, as it is shaped by knowing. And sometimes we need to see clearly beneath the surface—need to know. But I still wonder if in all of our technological advancements, in the use of sound waves to replace the human act of sounding, we are losing touch with the true depth of things in the world, losing the tangible connection between the leadsman's hands and the lead weight mapping the bottom. I wonder if we're losing mystery to the great wash of data.

Muckraking was the signature practice of so-called "yellow" journalists who scraped the bottom of the barrel in any story to dig up sensational or salacious, often fabricated details; and still today writers of nonfiction are often accused of dredging up the past and digging up bones. But sometimes such work has to be done. When someone disappeared without a trace in my Kansas hometown, at some point the decision was often made. When no other evidence appeared, suspicion turned to the Kansas River, or the Kaw as we called it, a name that evokes the sound of a crow's ragged cry but which was also a nickname for the Kansa Indians who originally inhabited the region. *Drag the river*, they'd say. Drag the Kaw. See what comes up. And the boats would motor into the river and drop their lines aft. The ropes, weighted with lead plummets and three-prong grappling hooks, or a metal drag-bar with steel teeth, spooled out behind as the pilots plowed a wake upstream, dragging the hooks behind them across the muddy bottom. When you drag the river, you aren't searching for a person any longer; you aren't trying to save a life. You are searching for a body. If you're lucky the body isn't knotted around a driftwood stump or pinned beneath a waterlogged tree. If you are lucky the body floated to the surface downstream and got stuck in an eddy current, swirling around with the flotsam and jetsam. Often rescuers never find anything and you have to wonder, try and fathom the disappearance of a person. That person was someone's child. Most likely that person was loved by another person, or at least by a loyal pet. The questions always swirl. The stories crested like a wave, pushing at the foundations of family and community. What happened? How did the person end up in the water? Where did s/he go? You don't think s/he tried to swim it? In the winter? But if the hooks bit into a body and the boats dragged up an answer, the truth of it would stretch the sounding lines taut like an awful big fish and you'd hear the boat's engine whine from the strain.

When a whale breaks for the surface, breaches, spouts, gulps in air, this is also called a *sounding*; whereas a *sound* in geographical terms—as in Prince William Sound or Puget Sound—finds it derivation from a different source and refers to a body of water, an inlet larger than a bay, deeper than a bight, and wider than a fjord. A bight is a shallow bay. A bite is a shallow stab at understanding, a sampling of a larger idea. I love the way language tries to capture the geography of thought.

To fathom, of course, also means to embrace, to wrap your arms around an idea and to understand, but the term is mostly used in the negative, to express a failure on the part of the speaker to grasp the meaning of something or, in a more generous, interpretation, to express a speaker's sense of wonder at what has been witnessed. Hardly anyone says, "I think I fathom what you're saying about cockles and whales." Instead you might say, "I cannot quite fathom how it all fits together," to which I might respond, "Yes, right. Me neither."

Or I might say: "But can you fathom what it would feel like to drown?"

And what I'd be saying is that it feels at times nearly impossible for me to wrap my arms around the enormity of a thing like the subject in an essay, nearly impossible to reach the emotional bottom without diving in too deep, without wallowing in the muck of sentimentality and nostalgia; and I'd be acknowledging the heavy angst of talking about a drowned boy and a man in a boat with a fish-finder.

I cannot fathom is a statement of the mind's failure expressed through the body's limitations, but it is also perhaps an expression of the failure of language, our primary vehicle for expressing our understanding of something. If you cannot fathom something then your arms are not long enough to find the words for it.

It was a hot day at the lake. We'd just wanted to cool off. We didn't see the boy slip under the surface.

Words still cannot reach this depth, not quite.

It's true. We dove down after him again and again. Blind in the muddy water, I swept my hands and legs out along the bottom, dragging my fingers through the muck for his body. But we never touched him. We couldn't see a thing until the man with the boat and the fish-finder showed up. The divers moved back. My friend and I had been joined by a crowd of six or seven, all of us diving down into the dark in search of the drowned boy.

The man in the boat stopped his boat and killed the engine. We all paddled around him in the water like ducks waiting for a peanut. A woman in a bikini yelled at us, "You need a buddy! Does everyone have a buddy?'

She meant a swim buddy. So nobody else disappeared. I looked at my friend. We'd known each other for fifteen years. We kept paddling while the man checked the monitor of his fish-finder. The minutes ticked by as he trolled slowly through the water. The boy had been underwater for at least twenty-five minutes. Suddenly the man in the boat leaned over the side and pointed at the water.

"Right there!" he said. "There's something big and it's not moving."

The divers all slipped beneath the surface, pushing for the bottom. One swimmer found the boy there in the mud. But he couldn't pull him up. They tried again. But it was too deep and the boy's lungs were already full. My friend and I were exhausted. We'd been in the water the whole time. We swam to the bank and sat down on the rocks.

Tiny waves cockled against the lakeshore.

The boy stayed on the bottom. He stayed there, the currents dragging on his body, until the Search and Rescue divers showed up a few minutes later. One of them in a wetsuit, mask, and air tank rolled off the back of the boat and disappeared. It seemed like he was gone a long time, but it was only a couple of minutes before he breached the surface, holding the boy's body.

I sat there and watched the scene unveil itself. I listened to the boy's body thump against the fiberglass hull of the rescue boat. And, honestly, I was surprised to see him at all. I feel terrible admitting this. But I think I had already committed to never knowing, never quite reaching the possibility of his death. I couldn't fathom how it would resonate through my consciousness, how these indiscriminate lines I now spool on to the page might bite into that day and drag it back up again. I couldn't fathom how I would still feel guilty that I couldn't do more. Part of me wanted to believe that the boy didn't actually die, that he would always exist below the surface of my thinking, like the ghost of an idea, as if he were just part of a story I tell again and again; but the thump of his body against the boat still reverberates up these sounding lines and rattles my grip on the present.

BIRD WATCHING IN FRESNO

Fresno, California 2008: In your new home, new neighborhood, a place your real estate agent described as "bohemian," you heard the ominous bird circling after dark like a sonic taunt, an auditory reminder of your tenuous existence in this place. The dark bird always overhead. You heard his watching. The omnipresent owl and his oscillating hum and buzz swirled above. It was strange here, this feeling of prey and this noisy bird hovering low over your neighborhood, searchlight swiveling and panning, casting day into the dark, the beam cutting through black yards, across rooftops, into bedrooms and your baby's room; and you just knew this bird would roost in the gum trees one night, perched outside your daughter's window, pushing its noise into her dreams too. The noisy bird's call rolled in waves around your family, slipping through open windows and running down the halls like some kind of angry ghost. It rolled over you in the yard in your big shorts and polystyrene gardening clogs, pushing you back into the shadows. Most nights you cowered under the mock orange tree or beneath the arbor and craned your neck out only when the bird circled around and away from the house, chasing after the skittering runners; the tweaking prey, the taggers and bangers; drunks running from cars, drunks stumbling out of bars. You watched the bird hover and spin and its wind pushed the guilty down like blades of grass, flattened them out on the asphalt. But the bird didn't see you in the backyard with your beer and your gardening clogs. Not you. Not those nights. The bird didn't suspect you yet, and besides it wouldn't chase what doesn't move, what has only recently roosted, relocated, separated and plugged into the seismic shifts of job, geography, and a new baby girl.

And the bird couldn't know how you felt caged by its noise, pressed and petrified like the prairie dogs back home in Kansas who ducked back into their holes when a raptor glided over the flats—even though you'd done nothing wrong, nothing but act like a prairie dog scratching in the yard. Some nights as your family slept, the stuttering beat of wings began to grate and worry you, insinuating itself into your thoughts, making you wonder if the bird had finally come for you, finally found some secret sin you didn't even understand. You wondered if your loneliness twitched like a rodent in the grass. And it was in these moments of weakness that you had the urge to call the bird home, to turn on all the outside lights, stand naked in the yard, beer bottle in one hand, and hoist your middle finger in the air, daring the cops to come. You would call their gaze down upon your head. And when your wail was drowned out in the chop of their witness, you'd bellow again, louder and longer, a supersonic scream that sent shock waves out and up into the air, the vibrations of your big noise rattling windows, shaking songbirds from their nests, whipping power lines like spaghetti noodles, until your own sound wave slammed into the helicopter and flipped it like a mosquito in a breeze, tumbling off into the stratosphere, the drone of it's blades fading to a whisper and then dying in the distance. Then it would be silent again. Then you might sleep. And you would act this way for no real reason, no reason other than the one which might explain why, as an awkward zit-faced adolescent, awake and alone in the house at night, afraid of your own reflection, you'd sometimes convince yourself that you were being watched, observed, spied on from the outside and judged; you'd pause before uncovered windows, your own face gawking back at you, winking from a distant more confident and comfortable life just out of reach, and you'd raise your middle finger to the other invisible eyes outside, each one lurking in the inky blue-black night. *Fuck you*, you'd say to no bird in particular. *Fuck you all.*

CROWN AND SHOULDER

Even here in California where there is little rain to speak of and few storm sewers, they still cut streets in the rough approximation of a human body—carved out of the hardpan, sculpted with a crown in the middle, sloping down into shoulders on each side to allow for drainage. Somehow this fact, this language of the body, seems wondrous to me, as all good facts can be, because it gives language and life to the common street, because it gives depth to the concrete and asphalt. Here's the thing: I *always* think about the bodies of streets. Especially the shoulders.

Most accidents on a street or highway happen in motion, speeding between the lines marking crown and shoulder. Most accident recovery and response on streets or highways, however, occurs on the shoulder, arrested in that liminal space, that in-between zone of vague boundaries and shifting definitions where motion is halted and disrupted, where we are invited to watch—but only for a moment. Most of what we witness, what we read, absorb, laugh or fear on the road occurs on the shoulder or just beyond its hazy penumbral boundaries. We pass by in our lane between crown and shoulder, brief patrons to a fragmented movie of moments; yet some of the most sublime and tragic, taboo, bizarre, desperate, scatological and lonely scenes of our lives and the lives of others zoom past us on these shoulders of streets, receding it seems into the irrevocable past of our memory—and it's troubling because the faster you try move past them, the more such moments stretch and blur into the present. This is the great paradox of rubbernecking: everything moves faster the closer you get. We slow our cars down trying to compensate for this. But the closer we get, the easier it is to see the details, the less time we have and the harder it is to see the whole picture.

When the Queen of England knights a man in modern times, she taps him first on the right shoulder with the broad side of a sword then raises it up and over his head and taps him on the left shoulder, again with the broad side. An embrace sometimes follows this ceremonial swordplay; and it is believed that these formal and mostly benign actions evolved from a more aggressive conferring of accolades. William the Conqueror, for example, is known to have knighted his son, Henry, by punching him squarely in the face.

Crown means tooth, cap and skull, but also means bestow, award, or honor; it is climax and triumph; it is the top of the head, a strike to the head, something golden and bejeweled you wear on your head; and in other intransitive verb forms: *as in a forest fire*, to burn rapidly through the tops of trees, and *as in pregnancy,* to appear at the vaginal opening. My forest-firefighter friend once told me that when a fire crowns, it roars jet-engine loud, trees boil from the inside and explode like giant Roman candles, raining sparks, flaming debris and melted pinesap, and the flames spread from tree-top to tree-top, dancing across the canopy. It is, he tells me, quite a show. Sometimes he just stands there rubbernecking at the terrifying beauty of it.

The neighborhood where I lived briefly in a famous poet's house is a tree-filled county island surrounded by the rest of Fresno. It's a strange anomaly, patrolled by sheriff's deputies instead of local police, a fiercely independent neighborhood that has steadfastly refused to join the city surrounding it even as it has been swallowed up by sprawl. As a county enclave, the neighborhood doesn't have street lamps or sidewalks, the shoulder improvements municipal tax dollars provide. Because of the darkness, it's a little dangerous to walk there at night. But it's also one of the nicest neighborhoods in town, filled with large homes on massive double or triple lots, most of them surrounded by the biggest, most regal eucalyptus, cedar, and redwood trees in the whole city. People like to walk there. It's almost like a suburban mall in the mornings, teeming with packs of active older men and women in sweat suits. You'll sometimes see a man walking with his bird, a large green and red Macaw perched on his shoulder. At night or early in the morning the walkers wear reflective clothing and headlamps or carry flashlights for safety. One woman straps headlamps to her dogs and the troop-of-them totter around in the predawn, their lights bouncing manically as they take up an entire lane or two of the street. In other neighborhoods, street shoulders are defined not just by the buzzing orange glow of streetlamps but also by sidewalks, those purposeful, sheltering slow-flow lanes of traffic that separate you from the push and howl of cars. In this neighborhood, where there are no lights and rarely anything at all besides dirt or encroaching grass and oleander shrubs, the pavement typically just drops sharply into the gutter or a ditch, or slumps into broken edges, ragged and rutted muddy patches, and trenches. Trees encroach on the public, tilting over the streets, green threatening to overtake everything. Still the pedestrians stroll, joggers jog, and people walk their dogs. Each year, hoards of tourists parade and stare at elaborate displays of Christmas lights twinkling in the redwoods; but they do all of this in the street and the lack of significant shoulders, sidewalks, or streetlights often feels oddly dangerous to me, amorphous and undefined in its boundaries, especially when I was walking with my kids, and

I found myself craving a consistent shoulder, something solid and broad, even and dependable, something to separate clearly the pedestrian experience from the driving experience.

Other intransitive verbs include *to rubberneck*, *to sleep*, and *to die*. Jesus died on the cross after being crowned with a wreath of thorns, and I have to admit I always liked this touch to the story. I appreciate the statues and paintings where Christ's blood is captured mid-trickle, snaking down from the crown onto his forehead and face. The gorier the Jesus, the better. Again and again as a child I wanted to hear how the Romans nailed him to the cross—one in each hand and one through both feet--and ran a sword through his side; but most of all I loved the irony of the crown of thorns, the not-so-subtle jab at his followers and at those who hoped to inspire future followers. I thought the Romans had a pretty wickedly comic sense of punishment; and believing this still, I sometimes imagine that because they really wanted to make a spectacle of Jesus, they nailed him up like a billboard, next to a roadway, perhaps on the shoulder of a major thoroughfare where the travelers could pause to gape at the sight of their King of King's death. It probably means I'm a terrible person, but I can clearly see the foot and cart traffic backed up for miles, donkeys braying in the heat, merchants cursing, and some poor soul at the back stuck in the rush hour, an unwitting victim to the rubbernecking instinct of weaker souls.

Sitting in a church pew on Sundays when I was a boy, I could almost feel Jesus's crown of thorns in my own scalp. But that might have just been the unrelenting boredom that I assumed was the definition of worship. Perhaps it was my own personal experience with the pain of religion and thorns. Church time came and went.

But hedge-apple thickets, protected by an armor of thorns, grew dense near the creek in the back of our house. I dealt with thorns every day, and one winter my little brother crashed his snow-sled into a thicket of them. When I raced down the hill and found him, a long brown thorn had pierced his nose from the side. He looked at me wide-eyed, then cross-eyed at the thorn in his nose, then back up, imploring me for help, but I just sort of shrugged. There wasn't really anything I could do. He barely made a sound. I told him to be careful. And I watched as he calmly tugged his flesh loose from the tangle. There was hardly any blood at first, but the thorn glistened a little wetter than the others. Afterward my brother staunched the wound with his glove and the two of us trudged home together through the deep snow.

Grief is an island, they say. In the intransitive form, *to grieve*, there is no object. In the passive voice, I *am grieving* and there's still no end. Or grief is Gilligan's Island; and no matter how many cosmonauts crash-land in the lagoon, I never get to leave. They never take me with them.

Or, grief is more like a virus that lives in your blood, something much more insidious than Ginger and Mary Ann, the Professor, Skipper and the Howells. It's something you have to shoulder forever, despite the false promise of closure. I know about viruses and how they can sneak up on you. In the summer of '99, camping in the mountains, a mosquito stung me. This mosquito carried a strain of viral meningitis; and two days later back at home, a fever washed over me. I vomited until my stomach was empty and didn't keep food down again until they hooked me up to an IV bag in the hospital a week later. In the midst of it, the meningeal layer between my brain and my skull flushed with infection and swelled, squeezing my brain until it felt like my eyes were being pushed out from the inside. I couldn't think straight, could barely talk or eat, and only managed to stumble from the couch to the bathroom to vomit and curl up on the floor. It took weeks, maybe months for my brain to recover. I lost over thirty pounds, and I lost my summer job waiting tables and tending bar at a Mexican restaurant because I tired easily, lost focus on the simplest of tasks, and couldn't remember the most basic order. Angry and confused at the outside world, I lost connection to people, retreated into my own head, a place still rocked and recovering from infection; I retreated into books and the written page. But this wasn't new for me. As a child I'd suffered febrile seizures that rendered me catatonic, nearly dead. I have vague, half-remembered, half-conjured images of waking in my father's arms in a cold shower, the streams of water hitting me like cold pellets. My parents recorded temperatures of 105 degrees or higher and the doctor's told them that I most likely lost some brain function, that I might end up being epileptic; and it's true that my seizures shared with epilepsy the terrifyingly euphoric rush of an unleashed mind speeding beyond time, but thus far the only affliction I can connect to my brain injuries is the writer's peculiar pathology, that push to see mystery in the mundane, an inflammation of perception I'm not sure I ever want to cure. Some days I wonder where I contracted this sickness. Other days I'm sure I know.

Many head injuries occur not because of direct impact of an object or fist to the skull but because the neck, rendered rubbery by the forces of gravity, snaps noodle-quick and the skull hits a hard surface like the tip of a bullwhip. Snap! The brain rattles around inside the boney cage like a clapper in a bell, which may be why in football, when you get hit really hard, they say, "you got your bell rung."

My father, a broad-shouldered man with an ursine presence, told me once, as an explanation for his support of suburban sprawl, "If they're not cutting streets, I don't have a job." At the time he worked as the manager of an asphalt plant owned by the same man who'd employed me in his excavation business as summer help many years ago. In a short time, Dad turned a money-losing operation into a profit-making operation. He spent his days in a modular trailer-turned-office and went to the bathroom in a port-o-potty. It was a job he described as "at the top of his physical abilities and the bottom of his mental abilities." When he started a business-consulting firm, I asked my dad what exactly he did for work, and he tried to describe his professional talents and skills. "I understand systems. Systems of all kinds and how things—information, products, whatever—move through that system. And I understand where they bottleneck, where the traffic clogs, and I understand how to fix those clogs."

To rubberneck is morally problematic partly because the intransitive action illuminates a conflict between the physicality of driving and the psychology of witness. It is more than morbid curiosity. To rubberneck is to indulge in subjectivity, into action without an object. It is morbid curiosity in motion, as if when confronted with a reason to rubberneck on the highway, we move from the light of objective reality into the darkness of subjective meaning-making and our senses instinctively dilate, gape open fish-mouth wide, and take in all the light possible before it's gone again, before we have time to really process what we've seen.

I've destroyed my shoulders. They're weaker than they used to be—worn down over time. The first obvious injury occurred during basketball practice my junior year. A sophomore guard stole the ball from me at the top of the key and raced down the court. I ran him down and as he laid the ball up, leapt into the air and pinned his shot against the backboard; but my momentum carried me underneath the basket, wrenching my arm back and behind me. I fell to the floor in agony and, for over a week, I couldn't lift my right arm without using my left one. I most likely tore my rotator cuff.

While snowboarding a few years later, I regularly had to catch myself from falling by extending my right arm out and kind of stiff-arming the snow or the occasional tree. Though I don't remember a specific injury, one night I removed my shirt to find a huge bruise leaking down from my shoulder, underneath my arm, and stretching its blue paint almost to my elbow. I still can't lift my arm over my head without some effort; and at night if I lie on my right side too long, my arm falls asleep. Sometimes my hand will go numb and tingle because scar tissue has impinged on my ulnar nerve. My nerve tunnels, the roadways for neural messages, are pinched and wounded, narrowing like a bottleneck of traffic, and it hurts sometimes when I try to lift my daughter into my arms.

You cut a street with a crown so the water will drain off, onto the shoulder, into the gutters. You cut crowns with a CAT brand or John Deere diesel-powered scraper, a machine descended from the original Fresno Scraper, a bladed street-carving tool named after the Central California town where it was invented, the city where I live. Fresno, California, is a place where crystal meth, homeless camps, car thefts, and foreclosures now make the national news, but where it's so much better and so much worse than anyone sees in such stories. Lately, many of the streetlights dotting the shoulders of the wealthier suburban neighborhoods have been rendered useless, casting vast stretches of city into darkness. The culprits, wire-thieves desperate for the money they can get recycling copper, open the light pole's access panel, snip the wire, and yank out as much wire as they can carry.

You shoulder a burden. The power. The responsibility. The load. The weight of things left unsaid. The darkness.

The head of a table is located at one chosen end, perhaps beneath a glowing glass cabinet of crystalline dishes and delicate porcelain figurines like a halo of stars. Are the sides then shoulders? Is the other end the ass of the table? The foot? The idiomatic phrase "giving the cold shoulder" refers broadly to an icy or unwelcoming reception and seems to come specifically from a passage of Sir Walter Scott's 1816 novel, *The Antiquary*, where he says, "The Countess's dislike didna gang farther at first than just showing o' the cauld shouther,"[8] while other etymological sources claim an origin in Andrew Reed's 1820 work, "No Fiction," describing the dinner gift of a cold shoulder of mutton: "How often have we admired the poor knight, who, to avoid the snares of bribery and dependence, was found making a second dinner from a cold shoulder of mutton, above the most affluent courtier, who had sold himself to others for a splendid pension!"[9]

Our bodies are built with shoulder blades. Our roads are cut with blades into crowns and shoulders. The Hormel Corporation makes SPAM, a pinkish canned meat product, from pork shoulder

---

8   http://www.phrases.org.uk/meanings/cold-shoulder.html
9   Reed, Andrew, "No Fiction," Oliver D. Cooke, Publisher, 1820, p. 194

and ham. Today, the intransitive activity, *to spam*, means to flood email in-boxes with unsolicited content, with images and advertisements that have no relevance to your life or interests. And it is often morbid curiosity that pushes the user to click on those links, those pathways to viral infection and worms that will shut down your systems or turn your computer into a zombie host. My email program has a "Report Spam" button that allows me to report suspicious emails to some mysterious spam-filtering authority. But the canned meat product for which this contemporary phenomena is named debuted in 1937; and if you visit the spam.com website you can find extensive details on the product's history and significance with colorful graphics, games, music, recipes, SPAM-related souvenirs, and even links to a local chapter of the SPAM fan club, where you can find information about SPAM festivals in your area, all of it unfiltered and un-ironic in its sincere love for canned meat.

SPAM is especially popular in Hawaii, where numerous "local" dishes feature it. I've never been there, but my father once traveled on business to Hawaii for an Asphalt Pavers convention. He went there because it was Hawaii, and he wanted to scuba dive; but he also went there, though he probably wouldn't admit it, to reconnect with my younger brother.

My brother had fallen love with the place during a high school science trip and always dreamed of returning. My dad, perhaps inspired by this, even bought into a timeshare on the Big Island; and, though I've never been there and my dad has since given up the time-share because of the prohibitive cost and time required when traveling from Kansas, for me nonfiction and Joan Didion's work doesn't get much more dense, dark and wonderful than her meditation on the living dead, "In the Islands."

One day on the 99, returning from the city, the intransitive *to slow* took on greater meaning. I slowed to a crawl in traffic. The kids were in the back seat, occupied with a movie or a toy. What was the hold up? Construction? Something on the shoulder? Cars creeping in both directions. Everyone rubbernecked as if there was a bad accident, slowing to crawl for no real reason other than morbid curiosity in motion. But there weren't the ambulances you expect, the fire engines—just a couple of highway patrol cars, a cop in the street, and an overturned truck, its trailer tipped over. A big yellow bulldozer shoved a pile of something. A pile of mud. A pile of sod. I saw the sod, the mud. Spilled on the highway. Spilled from the truck. But it wasn't mud or sod. It took me a second or two to realize. It was cows. Hoofs and heads. A pile of them. Thick black bodies, liquid as mud in their new death; and the bulldozer plowed them all into a roiling heap, a scrum of limp bovine bodies tumbling behind the insistent blade. Beyond the horizon of the pile, the silhouette of the overturned cattle truck loomed, wheels arrested. And everyone slowed their momentum to witness the spectacle, slowed knowing they'd seen something sublime, something that can never be repeated or recreated, could barely be described with words. In such moments, time becomes a function of thought. Time slows, warms to your intentions, becomes flexible and distends with meaning, inflating these moments in your memory until they are grotesque and monstrous with resonance.

Things that are seen on the shoulder of highways: cigarettes, piss bottles, fast food wrappers, shoes, underpants, bodies, dogs, cats, skunks, deer, red-tailed hawks in California, eagles in Alaska, evidence, secrets and other burdens too heavy to carry.

My father and I have both worked in the street-cutting business. In the summer of 1991, I took a job at the excavation company owned by a friend of my Dad's, the same man for whom he would later work when he ran the asphalt plant. I spent most of my summer driving a flatbed pickup with soft brakes and a temperamental starter motor, carrying a huge tank of diesel gasoline that I used to fill up all the company equipment. When I wasn't refueling, I operated a shovel and a wheelbarrow; if I was lucky maybe the Bobcat Uniloader, a small bulldozer used for a variety of odd jobs. Some days I'd spend hours working with a road scraper and operator, using survey stakes and a laser level to measure the grade from crown to shoulder. The scraper would carve, and I'd follow in the CASE Uniloader, bringing loads of dirt to fill in low spots the operator pointed out to me. Some days, the rattling hum of the Uniloader diesel engine would lull me into sleep and I would drift behind the scraper into the clay-orange-brown dreamscape of unfinished streets stretching out before me, houses sprouting amidst the promise map of a new neighborhood, new world, new reality, until some sound or shake would jolt me upright and I'd just miss crashing into the dirt, taking out the survey stakes and lines, ruining the soft shoulder.

When I say *to grieve*, I mean my response to the intransitive, *to die*. I mean my brother was killed on the shoulder of a road in Indianapolis, Indiana. He died there. And I mean the object, the transitive form of the verb. I grieve his death. I grieve the moments just after he and some friends had left the late showing of *Lethal Weapon* 3 and moved fast into the night, the moments just before his car skidded out on a turn, drifted across the crown line of the carved road . . . drifted over the white edged shoulder . . . and slammed into a tree. My brother's head snapped on his neck, slammed into bark and wood, his bell crushed, brain bruised and battered beyond repair. His friends survived with mostly minor injuries, but my brother died there in his car on the shoulder of some strange street in Indiana, his brain starved or flooded out. I don't really know the exact cause of his death.

I wonder how many people passed by that road's shoulder that night, May 16, 1992 in Indianapolis, slowed and turned their eyes to the scene. Who witnessed what I've only imagined? I can sometimes hear the noise of it in my head as clear as if I was there. But the images elude me. What was the rubbernecking like at the scene of my brother's death? What kind of tree killed him? Did it drop leaves or nuts or fruit on his car? How did he scar the bark? Was the light more orange-tinted or the bright white of halogen lamps? What could you see there in that theater of moments? These are terrible things to wonder. But still . . . I wonder how many people paused to consider the scene of my brother's death on the shoulder that night and what it means *to die* or *to grieve*, and how many others turned their heads away, back to the road ahead and kept moving, knowing what it means *to rubberneck*.

Though its etymological origins are unknown, it's possible that the *scapula* became *shoulder blade* because in ancient times, when a body had been rendered to bones, the scapula was then used as a digging tool. The bone-shovel turned the loam and clay then as the steel plow does today. Blades from bodies, fruit from soil, green from the rot.

I tell people all the time that my little brother was much smaller than me but always larger-than-life. I realize this is a cliché. I'm trying to be nice. What I should say is that my little brother had huge shoulders. He could carry loads I couldn't bear. But sometimes it's easier to speak to others about loss by trafficking in the low commerce of sentimentality. Such clichés become, I hope, at their best a kind of shared acknowledgement of the failures of language to adequately explain its own deployment in the name of essaying, exploring . . . just trying to make sense of things. I tell people that he was larger-than-life because the meaninglessness of the phrase represents an expression of the frustration I feel trying to explain my work—my writing or this essay—perhaps at my inability to stop rubbernecking at the past.

A Reiki therapist once told me, as an explanation for nagging shoulder and hand pain, that the right side of my body was heavier than my left, told me this might explain all the scars on the right versus the unblemished left, told me that we carry the burden of grief in the right side of our body. As she said this, I felt something snap and uncoil inside, as if her words had lifted the weight, if only for a moment. When I look in the mirror I'm sometimes convinced that my right shoulder is higher than the other, bound up and still knotted tight.

Some days I understand that everything I write is in some ways about my brother and his death. I realize in these moments that I'll never fully shake the weight of the loss, the object of the transitive form, *to grieve*. The essays may take on new forms, take new paths—this one trying to follow crowns and shoulders and rubbernecking, trying to be about physical injury, about the language of bodies--but they often (or always) end up back at the same old secret emotional engine, the humming grief that fuels so much of my creative life. I've shouldered the load for so many years; I forget it's there sometimes. My brother died on the shoulder of an Indiana street, crushed his crown against a tree; and I should have known that all of this essaying would tumble back down to this root, to his death, and that no matter how many digressive, gymnastic leaps I make, how many fancy roadside attractions I build for you, no matter how many cans of SPAM or other distractions I drop before you like shiny baubles in the margins of this essay, I can't escape the inevitable pull of gravity from crown to shoulder.

LAG TIME

Fresno, CA 2009: It doesn't thunderstorm in California. Not like those in my memories from home. I listen for them at night when the sky half promises, but it rarely delivers the noise I need. This I know: If you count the time it takes between the flash of a Kansas lightning bolt and the crack before the roll and peel of thunder. *If you time the lag,* Dad would say, *You can tell how close you are to the lightning.* He and I often lingered in the pre-storm, beneath a green-soup sky, dwelling in the pause between cause and effect. The neighbors too. All of us gawking at our potential demise, counting intervals between what was and what could be. And if there is an objective measure of a "split second" it would have to be close to the time between the flash of lightning and the sound of its ear-stunning crack, a noise that tingles up from your toes, and ripples through your belly—a sound the body hears before the ears; or maybe it is similar to that time I sat on the porch swing at the lake, and heard the lodge dinner bell ring itself, the clapper vibrating like an ear bone, a split second after a flash and strike to the metal tower; or the time between a blue racquetball's jump off the wall and the sound of its impact; or the gap between when your ear hears a noise in the house at night and the second your brain registers it as normal and safe (the sound of a dog dreaming, the rattle of the refrigerator) or something different, maybe dangerous (the wheezing croupy cough of your baby, the jiggling of a doorknob, a simple phone call in the middle of the night); or perhaps a split second is a more subjective measurement, the kind of tiny gap where I lose myself again and again in memory. Finally untethered, I drop this loss into the space between my father and me. I try to let go of that rip in his voice over the telephone almost twenty years ago, and the interminable pause after the words rolled out, *It's Matt. Your brother. There was an accident.* And just before the crack of the plastic phone receiver settling into its cradle, because in that lag, that brief second between what he said and the impact of what it meant, it was possible that things would always sound the same between us.

THE KING'S LAST GAME

Imagine this: It's early in the morning at the Graceland estate, well before dawn on August 16, 1977, just a few hours before the end, and the crickets and cicadas are thrumming in the Memphis heat. The sun is on the rise somewhere to the east, but the light hasn't yet reached this place. In the distance a small dog barks: sharp, rhythmically, and steady. A siren wails and fades. All else is quiet, all except for the strange noise emanating from an outbuilding behind the main house. It's a cacophonous noise. Unexpected. You creep up closer. Tiptoeing now like a trespasser, a voyeur. You shouldn't be here at all. Yet in this lucid dream you press your ear against the locked door and listen, straining to catch the strands of a voice. *The* voice. His voice. Perhaps you're hoping he might be playing a guitar, jamming with the band. But instead you hear an unexpected, but familiar, noise—the sound of a different kind of playing. It's the squeaking of shoes on hardwood, the *pop* and *twang* of a blue rubber ball rocketing off simulated catgut, followed by the resonant *crack* of it against a wall; and a different sort of music, that telltale *pop* and *pong* ringing out as the ball smacks off the back glass. You linger a while, listening to the high-pitched *slap* of a well-hit shot, and a short volley of forehand smashes going off like firecrackers. *Boom, boom, boom.* And laughter. Lots of laughter. Because the King is playing racquetball, and racquetball is fun. You know this game but not this side of Elvis, not this part of the story. This is your game, your father's game, a game of noise and speed. And more than anything you wish you could push the door open on that night and join the play.

* * *

90

Early that August morning, just hours before he died, Elvis Aaron Presley played his last game of racquetball. Elvis couldn't sleep, so he'd summoned his friends for a game. He asked for his favorite racquet, Red Guitar (named such because of the red guitar silhouette painted on the strings); and he asked his best friend, cousin Billy Smith, and Billy's wife to join he and his girlfriend, Ginger, on his custom-built court; all of them were apparently accustomed to such requests from the King. He wasn't sleeping much these days, and he got lonely late at night. Wouldn't you? Especially if your brain cranked with anxiety like a Cadillac engine? I know that feeling. It's not fun. He probably just wanted some fun, a distraction from the white noise of insomnia, that constant hum and drone of spinning thoughts.

It's hard to say for sure what exactly drew Elvis to the court that fateful night. Perhaps, like me in my late 30s and early 40s when I took up the game again, Elvis was seeking an escape. I like to think he too craved the *smash* and *slam* of a simple blue ball, the way it lets you forget the sludge of life. It *is* addictive. This leaving. This racquet play. This sideways step into music and sport. Because when the game is good, like a hit song, the court takes all the competing noise of the world, all the pressures and pain, and it absorbs them, shatters them and drowns them out in a cleansing blue noise. Every game is a dither, a rattle to your gauges.

Maybe Elvis appreciated such shaking, or maybe he just wanted a good laugh or a good rush before he died. Maybe he just figured all that exercise would help him sleep finally. Elvis took up the game after his wife, Priscilla, had an affair with Mike Stone, her Karate instructor and the couple divorced.

My own therapist suggested I take up some regular exercise to help with anxiety and the challenges of being a stay-at-home-dad and husband with two full-time jobs--Professor and Writer. Racquetball, she assured me, would make me happier, calmer, more peaceful. She told me it's a great stress reliever; and I have to admit that she may be onto something. The fitful nights and 4 a.m. wakeups, the feeding fun and the diaper rashes were easier somehow knowing I'd have the release of racquetball.

Regardless of the reasons behind Elvis's final request for a game of racquetball, it was hard to say no to the King, even at such an ungodly hour. His friends indulged him in a few games and afterward lounged around in the adjacent piano bar for a while. Elvis is said to have sung the last song of his life at this piano. Most people who have looked into this seem to agree that song was "Blue Eyes Crying in the Rain." After he finished, Elvis said goodnight to his friends, showered and changed out of his workout clothes, choosing a pair of comfortable pajamas. He crawled into bed next to Ginger and sat up reading a book titled *A Scientific Search for the Face of Jesus* by Frank O Adams.

When Ginger rolled over in bed a while later and cracked an eye, reaching a hand out to Elvis, he was still awake, still reading the Adams book. He told her he was going to the bathroom. Then Elvis got up, the book still clutched in his hand, and Ginger went back to sleep. She would never see Elvis alive again. They found the book on the floor next to his body.

Elvis died reading on the toilet—or at least he died very near the toilet. But according to most sources he died not from the 14 different drugs found in his system but from a fatal arrhythmia, a heart attack; and when I've told people that Elvis played racquetball just a short time before he died, many have wondered if racquetball killed Elvis. They wondered if the activity was too much for his addled heart. Mostly I think his death sounds so normal, so ordinary. He died of a heart attack while reading on the toilet. It could happen to any one of us.

Perhaps Elvis *was* taken down by the rhythm of racquetball, by a messed up beat or thump or bang in his heart brought on by the noisy ruckus of the game, or by the physical exertion of chasing that blue ball around the court. But I don't know about any of that, don't know the medical probabilities and don't really care. I don't care if racquetball killed Elvis. Because I'm pretty sure the game also let him live a little longer and a little fuller, if only for a couple of hours.

* * *

By most accounts, Elvis wasn't terribly good at racquetball. This did not, however, stop him from having his own court built at Graceland shortly after learning the game from the son of his trusted physician, Dr. Nick (George Nichopoulos), a figure just as controversial as Michael Jackson's notorious drug-dispensing doctor. But in addition to feeding him a steady diet of prescription narcotics, Dr. Nick was also, paradoxically, someone who was able to get Elvis to exercise.

Just as he was contributing to Elvis's decline he was also undoubtedly prolonging his life. You can't help getting exercise when you play racquetball. The game, even played halfheartedly, is an incredible workout, combining both cardiovascular and strength training; and, probably thanks in large part to Dr. Nick's prescribed activity, Elvis lost over twenty pounds and may have staved off all-out organ failure for at least a few months near the end of his life. If my therapist and many others are right about the ameliorative effects of regular exercise, it seems clear that the game probably also made the King a little happier.

Racquetball was also social for the King, something he shared with his most trusted friends, his posse of family and others

93

known to many as the Memphis Mafia. Along with a shared love of fireworks and booze, guns, and nice cars, the group also bonded over an appreciation for racquetball. Though the tales seem apocryphal, the King and his crew apparently played regularly around Memphis in the late 70s. Stories tell of the whole gang showing up en masse at a racquetball club for some fun, followed shortly thereafter by a crush of nearly hysterical fans; at least part of Elvis's desire to build his own court at Graceland was due to the public spectacle he and the Mafia caused on such occasions.

Elvis was said to harbor dreams of building racquetball complexes across the country; and though the Elvis Presley Racquetball and Swim Club, the King's Courts, or any other Elvis-inspired fitness center that I can dream up never actually materialized, the vision of private, urban, "everyman's" fitness centers was a dream that eventually came to fruition in many ways, much of it centered around the city of Memphis, Tennessee.

The USA Racquetball National Championships were held for fourteen consecutive years, until 2010, in Memphis, not far from Sun Records and a short drive from Graceland. Racquetball was just reaching the height of its popularity when Elvis played his last game in 1977. Nearly 14.5 million other people also played racquetball and in addition to the building of playground courts in inner cities, racquet clubs sprang up all across the country, ushering in a new era of the private athletic club, one that was much less elitist and suburban, much noisier, urban, and dirtier than the patrician tennis and golf clubs that had dominated the sports club scene in the 50's and 60's.

Racquetball courts were built next to basketball courts. They were built in cities, strip malls, and all over college campuses. They didn't need a ton of space like a tennis or golf club so they were adaptable. Women embraced racquetball, too, helping to make it one of the fastest growing sports at the time. Even kids like me soaked up knowledge of the game, taking lessons at the racquet club where our dads or moms played.

Unfortunately the 80s were as hard on racquetball as they were on fashion, rock music, and my parents' marriage. The good times did not roll on from the 70s; as the 80s drifted into the 90s—a decade marked by unprecedented growth and prosperity in America—the game of racquetball struggled mightily. By 2000 only about 4.5 million people worldwide were playing, a dramatic and precipitous decline in participation. Many health clubs converted court space into rooms for spinning, yoga, dance, kickboxing, or other group-exercise classes. Dad's old racquetball club is now a real estate office. Perhaps because health clubs became largely unaffordable to most Americans, or perhaps because other sports rose in popularity—extreme sports such as skateboarding and snowboarding—racquetball failed to attract young players and fell victim to shifts in age demographics.

In recent years, however, the pendulum has begun to swing back the other way. The sport has begun to gain popularity again and the US Open in racquetball has moved north, to Minneapolis, Minnesota, to a larger venue, the grand stage of the Target Center. Since 2000 participation has grown by about two percent every year, joining heavyweights like soccer and basketball as one of the few sports to increase its ranks annually. This may not seem like much until you consider that participation in "America's game," baseball, and in the ultra-cool extreme sport, skateboarding, *decreased* by as much as twelve percent over the same time period. The year 2008, a year defined by Barack Obama's message of hope, saw an astonishing eighteen percent increase in racquetball participation, with current estimates suggesting there are again over fourteen million people worldwide playing the game, just like when Elvis was alive and playing.

* * *

The truth is I'm more interested in Elvis's interest in racquetball than I am in the sensational details of his death or even his divorce from Priscilla, after she had an affair with her Karate instructor. I want to take a scalpel to all the details of the Elvis legend that don't matter so much to me. I want to cut away his troubled personal life, his rocky relationship with Priscilla and other women, or his rumored impotence and paranoia at the end, even his supposed tiff with his girlfriend, Ginger on the night he died. I can appreciate the stories of him giving away Cadillacs and playing with fireworks, but I have to admit that I'm only mildly interested in his music, appreciative of the early work and the occasional sing-along to "Viva Las Vegas" on a road trip. And I want to cut away the long list of drugs in his system when he died. I don't care whether he died on the toilet or next to the toilet or in front of the toilet, or whether his pajama pants were down or not, in part because I find such discussions humiliating and rather pointless, but also because in death we are all humiliated. Every death is an intimate experience and many (or more than we care to admit) of us die with our pants down, vulnerable, face first on the floor in front of the toilet. Hopefully we're reading better books than Elvis.

What I really care about is Elvis's decision, just hours before his death near his toilet, to play racquetball, a game that I love for many reasons, a game I can't stop thinking about. This means something, I'm sure. This small slice of shared experience. This common space between us, a racquetball court, was perhaps the last place he was truly alive in his body. At least that's what I like to believe. Though it's often overlooked, a sidenote to the more the salacious stories of that evening—such as Elvis going out at midnight for a dentist appointment, wearing a DEA jumpsuit, downing pre-packaged baggies of pills—the King's choice to play racquetball with his friends intrigues me more than any other detail of his life or death.

* * *

Much like rock and roll, racquetball is a hybrid invention created and marketed in the 50s in the United States by a few visionary individuals. Though he didn't give it its current name, Joe Sobek in Greenwich, Connecticut is widely credited as the inventor and marketer of the game as we know it. Sobek's goal was to create a faster, easier sport that combined elements of both handball and squash. Handball was hard on the body and squash was hard to master. Racquetball, a uniquely American amalgam of the two, became an instant hit in the YMCA where Sobek worked and at JCC's (Jewish Community Centers) and urban gyms across the country.

Racquetball and squash have very different personalities. In squash there are rules about where on the wall you can hit a shot, what walls you have to hit first, and what walls you can't hit first. My dad, who has taken up squash later in life, tried to explain the rules to me once, and it was as confusing as the day he tried to teach me how to play cribbage.

Racquetball is different. The rules are easy to master because there are relatively few of them. In racquetball every wall is in play. Everything's fair game. More significantly, however, is the existence in racquetball of the "kill shot." This shot is the ultimate expression of power and skill. The "kill shot" is an unreturnable shot that hits low on the wall, sometimes right at the crack where wall meets floor, and then dribbles out, impossible to return, effectively "killing" the ball's momentum and the opponents chances. Racquetball racquets are rated according to their "kill-shot power," and much of the game's strategy is focused on setting oneself up for the shot.

In squash there is no kill shot. They are forbidden by the rules of the game. This difference alone defines much of the difference between the two games. To put it in other terms, squash is a strategic dance, a game of finesse and strength, like a waltz competition with a partner. Racquetball is more like competitive slam dancing to speed metal. It's a game that emphasizes individualism, power and force, speed and aggression. The sport is as quintessentially American as rock and roll, apple pie, monster trucks, and Elvis.

* * *

Despite the outward show of brute power, racquetball is also, at its core, a game of precise skill. The best players are those who can harness the energy and laser-focus it at an ever-moving blue target. Like playing pool, once you learn the angles, learn how to place a kill shot or set yourself up several shots in advance, there's little in terms of hustle, work, or luck that's going to help your opponent. That's why you have to watch out for the crafty old men at the gym, the slightly overweight guys whose knees quit years ago but who can fire off a wicked Z-serve or snap a forehand kill shot to the front-wall crack with astonishing and humiliating regularity. It doesn't matter how young and fast you are, if you can't return a serve you can't break a serve and can't score any points of your own.

Elvis was forty-two when he started playing the game in the wake of a separation and divorce. I'm in my early forties now, and I started playing racquetball again recently after taking a couple of years off. I play now in spurts of activity when I have the time or when I can find someone who will play with me. I'm not far from being the crafty old guy at the gym. I have bad knees, at least one messed up shoulder, and I'm Sasquatch-slow. But if there's a positive, it's that I'm blessed with long, simian-like arms and a decent understanding of how that frantic blue ball bounces and moves through space. I've also come to understand the importance of patience. In racquetball, you have to let the ball come to you. You have to watch the ball and not crowd it. You can't impose your will upon the ball because it will not bounce to your wishes. You can spend all of a game chasing that thing into corners, and it will always move faster than you, always bounce in ways you can't predict.

* * *

Elvis played racquetball with his friends, but it's not clear if his posse really enjoyed the game or just enjoyed being around Elvis. Sport, even causally enjoyed amongst friends can be a test, a tug at the bonds that define your relationship and your identity. Most of us have had those experiences where fun suddenly turns competitive, where one guy takes a game too seriously and the whole dynamic shifts. That guy was usually me.

But what if that guy was Elvis? Play always has the potential to drift into something where skill, power, and artistry, or simple competitive fire, transcend the bonds of friendship, family, or society. Despite it's association with childhood innocence, play is inherently risky and, therefore, also inherently rewarding. What if Elvis was the super-competitive dude in Rec-Specs hopping around the court, bellowing at blown shots or hollering when he hit a kill shot? What if he kicked your ass in racquetball AND rock and roll? So much has been said about Elvis, his music, his life and the minutia of the night he died. His death has been canonized.

But what can be said about Elvis's last game of racquetball?

If we're to trust the stories, Elvis's final game wasn't the display of physical artistry I like to imagine but instead quickly deteriorated into a free-for-all game of dodgeball where Elvis hit balls at his friends and girlfriend, Ginger, laughing at their discomfort like some kind of bully. It's possible tempers flared and a racket or two was thrown.

This troubles me. It suggests to me that the game didn't mean to Elvis what I want it to mean, that racquetball was just something to do, something to help him sleep, or worse a way for him to feel powerful again. Fans and biographers seem, however, to worry more over what songs he sung at the piano bar or what he said to Billy or Ginger or anyone else that night; or they worry about the list of drugs he ingested, the clothes he wore, the book he was reading. Few people seem to worry as much about the King and his racquetball court, this temple of noise and energy, and how he played his last game. Part of me wants to rescue the King from that image of a bully or buffoon on the court. I want to believe he was better than the stories.

* * *

Now imagine this possibility: It's late at night and the moon is so fat it might croak. You're back again at the Graceland of your imagination. Listening. Trespassing in the past. Up to this point you've engaged with Elvis mostly as a pop-culture construct, a caricature only amplified by the other sensational details of the night he died; and because such constructs are malleable as clay, you know you can shape them into your own solipsistic idea, can make them better, or at least make them your own in some way. So let's pretend it's maybe a day or two before the King kicks the bucket, well outside the penumbra of the spotlight on August 16.

Elvis is up again, unable to sleep, and he's playing racquetball to relax and have fun. Perhaps this time you've found your way inside the court. Perhaps you've moved beyond the glass that separates the two of you. Elvis swings at a bouncing blue ball. He's wearing a white tracksuit with yellow piping and blue stripes stretching down the sleeves and legs. He's wearing a headband and swinging his Red Guitar racquet. He's laughing at you in your baggy shorts and your headband. You're playing racquetball with the King, if only for a serve or two.

Though it's hard for him to hit them with any regularity, Elvis clearly appreciates the focus and precision of a kill shot, hit low to the floor, and the music and geometry of the long, looping shots that strike high and pinball around the upper walls. Sometimes when he can't get to a shot to return it, he'll just watch the ball bounce, tracking it like a bird dog, listening to the sound of it. This is something the two of you can share, this appreciation for the noise and movement of the game.

Elvis smiles a lot when he's on the court, clearly soothed by the *squeak*, *squeak* lullaby of shoes on the hardwood, a *slam* of soles, even the visceral *grunts* and *barks*, the hip *crashes* against the walls. You can see that Elvis loves the noise of the game just like you do, loves the *bwong-snap* of a forehand smash, the artillery-like racket of sound, and that special trick of physics that lets you hear the ball hit the wall a split second after you see it.

He's big enough to seem like a bully, but that's not how Elvis carries himself in his court, not on this night. You don't want to infantilize him but there is something distinctly childlike and unself-conscious about Elvis in this space. He's playing, really playing, and perhaps he enjoys your failures a bit much. Perhaps he laughs when you swing and miss. Maybe he tries to hit you with the ball a couple of times just for kicks. But he's jamming right along, making some noise with you. He's not great and wouldn't have lasted long in a real game with your dad or even with you if you were playing hard; part of you wants to give him some tips, to teach Elvis a couple of things about the game. You want to talk about patience and focus. You want to talk about discipline. You want the game to save him. He's still out there, alive and running around, swinging his Red Guitar and having fun. You can hear his shoes squeaking on the wood. You can hear it all, especially the way the acoustics of the court seem to rescue his voice from the excesses of his life; it booms deep and resonant and new again, and you think you could listen to him play all night long.

* * *

The greatest seduction of any sport is that it convinces both players and fans that the stakes are nothing less than survival. Each game matters because it cannot be duplicated, cannot be revised or practiced until it is perfect. It is a spontaneous expression of a practiced skill. This is perhaps one difference between play and performance, between game and song.

A game of racquetball at its best is like a band jam session. It can only be played that way once. Each session, despite it's chaotic and improvisational potential, is still shaped by specific mutually agreed upon conventions, shaped by accepted boundaries and rules. Each rewards skill and technique and includes at least some element of competition, and each also requires some vulnerability, some shared space and a deep love of noisy play.

By 1977, Elvis was forty-two and perhaps long past jamming with a band. He didn't play songs so much as he performed them. Elvis's choice to play racquetball was in some way perhaps a choice to jam, to let go of the constant performance of his Elvis identity and to improvise on the court. It was a choice to play a different kind of music. I say this because I don't want to believe that the game simply matters because it was his last game, just something he did, and important only because it preceded the last songs he sang.

I think that as much as Elvis loved racquetball, it must have pained him to know he couldn't control it completely. It had to be both frustrating and exhilarating for him to subject himself to the rule-bound chaos of the game, to surrender to an experience that had the potential to expose his weakness and vulnerability. Perhaps Billy aced him on a couple of serves, or Elvis fell on his face diving for a shot. Maybe they laughed at him. Maybe Elvis looked silly or clumsy and, as much as we all need permission to feel that way sometimes, it must have also been hard for his friends to see, hard to contain or reconcile with the other Elvis they knew. This kind of dynamic might explain the rumored tension during the King's last game. It might explain flaring tempers and thrown racquets.

For the sake of argument, though, let's suppose that in the hours before he died, Elvis chose to surrender some part of himself to the game, to let go of his inhibitions and really play; and let's imagine that Elvis was at least capable of hitting the ball really hard, if not equally capable of a decent serve. Even if that last game didn't work out perfectly, does such an image of Elvis change the story of that night? Does his last game, however it was played, make the King's last breath more or less tragic?

I don't know. But I do know that for me this fact, his choice to play racquetball, makes the story of that night much more interesting, much deeper and more complicated. The simple fact—Elvis played racquetball shortly before he died—somehow makes him less of a caricature, less pop culture construct, and more real, more honest and human. The choice to play is perhaps more noble and humble than at first it seems, and more complicated than many other choices Elvis made that night. The choice to play is a choice to survive, to thrive and feel the noise of the game.

Though I've never visited Graceland and must admit to feeling no great desire to do so, I would like to see the racquetball court—or what's left of it. Apparently the court was long ago converted into a museum displaying his gold and platinum records. You can't rent a racquet and ball and hit some shots on the King's Court. I wish. In my imagination the court *is* a kind of temple to the playful creative King, to the inventive, imaginative, and improvisational Elvis, and I like to think I could stand there now, surrounded by his records of success, and hear the ghost noise of his last game still echoing off the walls.

ON LOITERING

"If we do not keep (our minds) busy with some particular subject which can serve as bridle to reign them in, they charge ungovernably about, ranging to and fro over the wastelands of our thoughts . . . Then, there is no madness, no raving lunacy, which such agitations do not bring forth."
  – Michel de Montaigne, "Of Idleness"

1.

In Charles Moore's iconic black-and-white photograph, Coretta looks on stoically, lips parted, hands clasped in front as her husband, Martin Luther King, Jr. has his right arm bent behind his back by a police officer in a tall hat. Someone unseen, outside the frame, places a hand on Coretta's left arm, as if to comfort or contain her. Martin pitches forward over a counter, leaning to his right, his left hand splayed out for support on the polished surface. He wears a light-colored suit and tie, a panama hat with a black band. The force of the officer's grip has nearly yanked the jacket off his right shoulder. The officer's left hand pushes against Dr. King's left side, bunching up his jacket, shoving him forward, bending him over the counter. Another officer stands behind Martin's right shoulder but you can only see the top of his hat and his right arm resting casually on the counter. A hatless white officer stands behind the counter and our perspective peers over his right shoulder into Dr. King's face. Martin doesn't look pained. Resigned perhaps, sadly familiar with this sort of treatment. The man behind the counter seems to be reaching out with his left hand to take something or give something (a piece of paper perhaps) from Martin as his right arm blurs at the bottom edge of the frame. Martin, his eyes pulled all the way to the right, is either looking at the man behind the counter or at someone else we can't see. The date is September 3, 1958 at the Montgomery County Courthouse in Alabama. Martin Luther King, Jr. is there to support his longtime friend, Ralph Abernathy, a Baptist minister testifying in the trial of a deranged man charged with chasing Abernathy down the street with a hatchet. In the photo King has just been arrested for loitering. He will spend fourteen days in jail as punishment for his crime. The strange thing is that in Moore's photograph it is not Martin or Coretta who look afraid. It's the policemen who appear flustered and scared. The photo is superficially silent. But you can still see how blurry with fear they are of his power and presence, quivering before his radical subjectivity in that space.

2.

Loitering is not particularly difficult or physically demanding. It doesn't, at first blush, appear revolutionary or criminal. Consider that "loiter" is an intransitive verb. There is no object to it. It is all subject and subjectivity. To loiter requires simply that you stand around or sit aimlessly, without purpose, to choose a space because it happens to be in the shade, or just happens to be there. Anywhere. The key to pure loitering—the most honest embodiment of the word's spirit—is of course to do nothing. Absolutely nothing.

But it has become bigger than that. Revolutionary. To do nothing now in the name of loitering is also now to repurpose, in the name of purposeless, an otherwise purposed space. And we are surrounded by purposed spaces. To loiter then is a kind of Zen-like appropriation, a subjective possession of objective, though often marginal, space, and perhaps this is enough to make it revolutionary, enough to threaten those who are invested in the purposing or owning of such space. It worries us when someone does nothing, even when they seem to be doing nothing on a street corner, a roadway median, an alley, or some other marginal space. We're so busy, so purposeful; in our world of increasing technological connection, we're always engaged in some activity. It's hard for us to understand the idleness of loitering. It frightens us. On some level we tend to believe the aphorism, "Idle hands are the Devil's playthings," and associate the nothingness of loitering with all manner of bad or dangerous possibilities, even with the potential for actual evil.

Even one of history's greatest loiterers Michel de Montaigne, the father of the modern essay and a man who spent a great deal of time walking around his estate and thinking about the stuff of everyday life, recognized the danger of too much idleness. In his essay, "Of Idleness," he acknowledges that he'd, "retired to his estates, determined to devote myself as far as I could to spending what little life I have left quietly and privately," giving his mind the "greatest favour" of "total idleness," but instead found that, "it gives birth to so many chimeras and fantastic monstrosities, one after another, without order or fitness." Montaigne uses the extended metaphor of a horse throughout the short, two-page essay to define the tendency of a purposeless mind to run wild, "ranging to and fro over the wasteland of our thoughts," and gives us perhaps a brief exploration of why we find loitering so full of dangerous potential.

Part of the trouble is that it is nearly impossible to define "doing nothing" from "doing something." Even when my car's engine is idling, the car still creeps forward, still moves. People who truly loiter assume a kind of vague and amorphous, but still frightening, potentiality. They are idling engines. The ambiguity of their physical and moral position troubles us. After all, when is any one of us actually doing nothing in any space? Have you ever truly done *nothing*?

Montaigne was clearly able to overcome the mad pull of idleness and bridle his runaway mind enough to write well over a hundred essays. Even when I putter around my yard or sit on my front porch, thinking about whatever I'm currently writing or reading, aren't I still doing something, even if that something is only thinking? Essays, composed and constructed often in such moments of idleness when I have the space and time to do nothing, become a kind of harness as well, a way to focus my ranging mind. But as long as I'm essaying in my house, or at my desk, even in a coffee shop or a bar, I'm still using the space with an intent that seems to fit the space. I wonder how long I could loiter on my street corner, just stand around thinking about an essay I'm working on, watching people and traffic without drawing unwanted attention to myself. I wonder if that time would be different if I lived in a wealthier, gated community on the North side of town, one of those places where they don't really have street corners. What if I just stood around in the middle of a cul-de-sac and told anyone who asked that I was just thinking about some stuff? Or if I lived in a more poverty-stricken, gang-controlled neighborhood in a different part of Fresno would my loitering embody a different potentiality? Of course it would. I wouldn't have the luxury of rumination. The objective nothingness in my loitering allows my subjectivity to be shaped to the expectations of the context.

Loitering, as an idea, is as undefined, abstract, and subjective as happiness or suffering. It can be adapted and appropriated, shaped to fit the situation; and then laws or ordinances or signs that attempt to regulate loitering are the ontological equivalent of ordinances regulating or controlling happiness or suffering. They are perhaps the most common legislative manifestations of the conflict between subjective intent and attempts at objective measurement of said intent.

Sometimes I think about this when I visit the Food King market in my neighborhood, a subjectively happy place, a true neighborhood convenience store. It feels like home to me. I don't even care that it costs me nearly twenty dollars for two six-packs of beer. The brothers, Mo and Najib, who own the Food King, emigrated to the U.S. from Yemen and are exceedingly nice to me, always calling me by name. They know *most* of their customers by name; sometimes Najib's bespectacled son sits behind the counter working on his homework. Mo and Najib often talk about the weather and they're usually listening to NPR on the radio. But they also have prominent "No Loitering" signs posted on the front of the store and a bank of video monitors that allow them to keep an eye on every part of their property. You have about as much time to linger in front of the Food King as you do in front of an airport. Pause too long and you will be hustled along.

Mo and Najib have to deal with challenges I can barely imagine. Fresno is a dangerous place filled with desperate people. Nobody denies this reality. We just live with it. But Mo and Najib run a tight ship, more than most places. They keep their store clean and free of the crowds that loiter around elsewhere. They never hesitate to chase off the street-kids and panhandlers, the tweakers and the prostitutes; and I have to admit I appreciate this, that it makes me feel somewhat safer as a consumer.

When I asked Mo one day about his "No loitering" signs and how he enforces the rule, he told me that he just tells any loiterers to move along, and if they don't move, he might threaten to call the police.

"But would they come?" I asked.

"Yeah, sure. Maybe. But if you just mention the police, they mostly move along."

"And if they don't?"

"If they don't, I take my stick out there and tell them I'm gonna count to three, and then I'm gonna hit you with this stick."

Mo didn't show me his stick, but I guessed it was some kind of baton. I didn't doubt his conviction. Mo meant business. To him the issue is all black and white, no gray area, no room for interpretation. This is his property, his Food King, and he is in charge of defining loitering in this subjective space. He also told me he has a gun under the counter, if it came to that.

Perhaps the most extreme example of the threatening potentiality of loitering is in the context of an elementary school, an exaggeratedly purposed and morally charged public space. If you stand around outside the playground fence of a school, just stand there, long enough, most likely your loitering will be seen as a threat and you will most likely be confronted by authority figures. In Fresno six-foot chain-link safety fencing surrounds all the public schools. If you're loitering around a school, regardless of your intent (maybe you're studying the architecture of schools for a class) you might be arrested or at least hassled and hustled along. There are signs posted everywhere forbidding all manner of activities, including dog walking, golfing, model-airplane flying, and loitering; and as a parent of elementary school children, I'm glad to see those signs when we take our dog there for walks. I don't really care if you're flying model-airplanes at my daughter's school, but I do care if you're loitering there. It doesn't matter to me if you're innocently researching something for a novel or an essay, maybe snapping photos with your iPhone, I just want you to move along and take your subjectivity elsewhere. An elementary school is a place where the objective truth of the context overwhelms the subjective truth of anyone who moves through the space. Your rights are necessarily limited there, and it doesn't end at the fence. The rights-defining power of an elementary school space extends well beyond the fences, past the sidewalks, into the streets, where the rules of driving are more stringent and more morally charged, and even further beyond into surrounding neighborhoods, where legal penalties for things like narcotics trafficking are increased. In such spaces the objective meaning of the place overwrites your subjective intent.

It is also the vague undefined nature of loitering combined with the impossibility of truly knowing or measuring subjective intent that has allowed anti-loitering laws and ordinances to be used as a weapon against civil disobedience. Martin Luther King was arrested because anti-loitering laws on the books in Montgomery allowed the police, regardless of the facts of that day, to define King's presence, to shape his intent into something criminal, something they could use to control him. He was merely attending a public trial. But anti-loitering laws allowed the police to arrest him for being black in a white space.

Attempts to criminalize loitering have been used more recently to try to control gang activity, drug sales, panhandling and prostitution, as well as to control populations of homeless people and protesters in the nationwide Occupy movement. These efforts, though often temporarily successful, are often doomed to failure, perhaps because of the very nature of loitering itself. Courts have recognized that anti-loitering laws often encourage racial profiling and police abuse of marginalized groups. Legislating loitering is like legislating nothingness.

In February 2012 New York City settled a class-action lawsuit brought on behalf of thousands of citizens arrested over the years on anti-loitering charges that had been deemed unconstitutional. The city's efforts to control loitering over a span of thirty years will ultimately cost them fifteen million dollars and require them to expunge thousands of arrests and convictions. There is little evidence to suggest, however, that this will change the way anti-loitering laws and ordinances are used to control marginalized populations in this country. We are simply too purposed and possessive of our objective spaces, too frightened by the potential of loiterers.

In other communities, perhaps due to the challenges of defining and enforcing anti-loitering ordinances, business owners are turning to less obviously confrontational, more passive, subjective, and subliminal deterrence methods. They're turning to sound warfare as a way to avoid the whole messy enterprise of objectively measuring and legislating against subjective intent. Perhaps they're doing this because it protects them from images of abuse and violence and the cultural resonance created by such pictures.

5.

The Mosquito was invented in Wales several years ago.

Moving Sound Technologies has been marketing and selling the Mosquito throughout North America. Many cities, municipalities, school districts, and parks boards use the Mosquito to combat vandalism

The patented Mosquito is a small speaker that produces a high frequency sound much like the buzzing of the insect it's named after. This high frequency can be heard by young people 13 to 25 years old.

The latest version of the Mosquito is called the MK4 Multi-Age. It has two different settings one for teenagers 13 – 25 years and one setting for all ages.

When it is set to 17KHz the Mosquito can only be heard by teenagers approximately 13 to 25 years of age.

When set to 8 KHz the Mosquito can be heard by all ages.

In case you thought Mosquito is all about annoying sound that would force the loiterers to run for cover you would be in for a pleasant surprise!

The Music Mosquito is a complete music system that will relay Royalty free Classical or Chill-out music that would keep the teenagers away to some extent.

Mosquito has a strong steel body . . .

Mosquito anti-loitering device is a handy option to suppress vandalism and the issues of graffiti aggressively.

The Mosquito Device can help with Teen Loitering Problems.

Mosquito has a strong steel body . . .

The Mosquito Device can help with Gang Loitering Problems

Mosquito has a strong steel body . . .

The Mosquito Device can help with Vandalism Problems

Mosquito has a strong steel body . . .

The Mosquito Device can help with Grafitti[10] Problems

Mosquito has a strong steel body . . .

---

10   Sic. All italicized passages taken from the Moving Sound Technologies website. Moving Sound Tech, 2012, http://movingsoundtech.com/.

6.

At night now in Fresno, or maybe in your city, they gather beneath the glow of streetlamps, lurking around its penumbral cone of light, the ghetto birds fluttering overhead. Packs of teenagers. Black kids. Brown kids. White kids. Brawny boys in baggy clothes, hats and team jerseys; pale, inked kids wearing white wife-beaters; girls in skinny jeans, high-heels and higher hair; or a population of bearded men smiling through meth-snaggled teeth; shuffling burn outs and tweakers with face tattoos; gang bangers with bulldog paws or red lips painted permanently on their necks; or maybe it's those ubiquitous kids at a suburban mall wearing Polo shirts and skinny jeans, high-top sneakers, and puffy ski jackets, and they're loitering around Jamba Juice or the movie theater, around your neighborhood school, or outside your business every night. These are the loiterers, the idle enemies of consumption and purpose. These are the targets of subjective warfare.

In my Kansas hometown, the high school kids from outlying rural communities used to drive to downtown Lawrence, park their trucks backwards in the diagonal spaces along Massachusetts St. and set up lawn chairs in the beds. They watched the rest of us stroll past as if we were specimens in museums. Often we looked the part. Often things were said. Often there were fights. Often there was litter and vandalism. In response, several merchants installed strobe lights in the windows of their stores, leaving them on all night long as a kind of annoyance, an agitation of the space and a passive form of loitering enforcement. It worked, too. After a while nobody wanted to park or linger in front of those shops. There were fewer fights there, less litter and vandalism. But the lights also just made the business owners seem mean and intolerant.

It doesn't matter, really, what loiterers look like for the purposes of the Mosquito or for a strobe light. Such passive forms of loitering deterrence don't discriminate on the basis of color, class, caste, or clothing choice. They cannot violate rights, in part because we have few clear legal protections against noise or light pollution, despite its obvious influence on subjective experiences of happiness or suffering. Noise might not violate your rights. It can't bend you over a counter and handcuff you, but it can violate your space and subjectivity. It can make it hard to think, even hard to do nothing.

What matters to the Mosquito is not the motivations of the loiterer, but simply that the subjective loitering body courses with blood and has ears with which to listen. In this way it is much like a bomb. A very smart bomb. What makes the Mosquito insidious is how it targets the age of the loiterer, his youth and the way his brain processes sound. Imagine a bomb that only wipes out people of a certain age, a bomb that targets only the young. The Mosquito doesn't care about the kinetic potential for chaos, for unpredictable behavior inherent in the loiterer's stasis. It doesn't care about anything, because the Mosquito is a machine designed to create an automatic physiological response, because its intrusion into your subjective internal space is silent, indiscriminate, and subtly violent.

The danger of loiterers at rest is that bodies will remain at rest until acted upon by an outside force. The danger is the malicious pull of idle hands toward evil deeds. And the popular imagination associates loitering—a behavior defined specifically by its purposelessness—with all sorts of bad or illicit purposes; most notably property crimes like vandalism and graffiti, as well as gang activity and prostitution. And because there is often little else for them to do, no other place for them to gather, teenagers—the ultimate in-betweeners—are regular offenders of anti-loitering efforts and ordinances. By their very nature, teenagers embody the conflict between objective rules and expectations and subjective intent. They live perpetually in the liminal space between outside rules and their internal wills. Teenagers are all subjectivity, all solipsistic fervor; they are in essence loitering between childhood and adulthood, embodying that marginalized space with intent that is often inscrutable to those of us living outside that space.

In my neighborhood, the loitering teens move between a series of spots, these odd in-between places like the island of a parking lot behind Starbucks and Bobby Salazar's Mexican restaurant, or someone's yard, perhaps the community garden, up against the brick wall of the Brass Unicorn and the Starline or in the side yard of an apartment building on Maroa Ave. You won't find them outside the Food King, but nearby in side streets and alleyways, lounging in various liminal spaces.

Much to the chagrin of many Fresno shoppers we also find loitering teens on the wealthy, north side of town at the clay-colored strip mall called River Park, a palace to consumerism and multi-national corporations that, in an effort to curb loitering, not long ago tried to ban unaccompanied teenagers from the premises. That didn't work so well.

A parent or other objectively recognized adult had to be with any teenager on the premises. It wasn't clear how the mall intended to enforce this—if they planned to randomly ID anyone who looked young enough to be a teenager. Perhaps they simply should have installed Mosquito anti-loitering devices in the same places they've installed Muzak speakers and security cameras. We fear teenagers not because of their loitering itself—that gray penumbral area between right and wrong—but because the act of doing so suggests, by its mere existence, the possibility for harm, for mayhem and destruction. We fear their unbridled youth and all of its sublime potentiality. We fear their marginalized status because it lives outside the boundaries of our control.

One day not long ago, as I was driving home from lunch with a friend, I took a side street that parallels a major thoroughfare, a street known as a popular hangout for the Fresno street kids and the homeless. A homeowner who has been working on remodeling a large house that backs up to the street recently installed a painted wooden fence and stacked-stone planters surrounding mature pomegranate trees. He's created a lovely little oasis of landscape architecture that would appeal to nearly anyone's aesthetic; and as I drove past this oasis, I saw a loose pack of loitering teens lounging around the planters, smoking, pawing at each other, laughing, and doing nothing. All of them. Loitering. Just sitting there, doing nothing. And I felt this momentary urge to yell at them or drive them away somehow, but I wasn't sure why. Perhaps it was jealousy. Perhaps it was fear.

Unless I'm writing or reading, I have trouble sitting still for ten minutes. I can't imagine doing it for two or ten hours. I wondered if the homeowner might want to think about getting the Mosquito anti-loitering device, if he might want to agitate their space and send out high-pitched squeals of deterrent noise. I thought this might be something I would do if I owned the house, but even as I thought it I cringed at the idea, the invasion and violation of space, as well as at the aesthetic and moral cruelty of creating an otherwise appealing place that would be simultaneously physiologically repulsive, a space whose 17 MHz of Mosquito noise would hurt the ears of young people.

These days when teenagers loiter across the street from our house, making out or smoking weed from a can or a pipe or a blunt wrap, I mostly ignore them. Some days I want to tell them to move along or to smoke somewhere else. Some days I want to warn them that other people aren't so understanding, that the police often patrol our street since it's so close to the high school. But the most I ever do, if I'm out front with my kids, is give the teenagers a hard stare, maybe a wave to let them know I see them, to suggest they might move along.

I've thought about calling the police, but the Fresno police frighten me more than loitering teenagers. They shoot people. Pretty regularly. I don't want these kids to get shot or even arrested. And besides I don't really want to be *that* guy—the asshole neighbor who calls the cops on kids. The truth is they're not hurting anyone, except maybe themselves. They're just hanging around because they can, because they have nowhere else to go. My friends and I did similar stuff in high school. We used to drive out into the Kansas countryside, down empty gravel roads, to find space where we could smoke or drink. These kids like to linger against the tall fence along my neighbor's side yard and sit beneath the overhanging tree on the stacked railroad ties. It's only a block from Fresno High School, away from the crush of other kids and just beyond the boundaries of school space. It seems safe enough, like a place they can loiter in peace.

Who am I to deny them this space?

I watch them sometimes, and I think about Mo and his stick, his gun under the counter. I think about the Mosquito, and I wonder how I would react if the teenagers crossed the street, crossed the line, and started loitering in my yard, if they even got close to my daughter and invaded my subjective space.

I'm not sure I would even count to three.

I like to think I'm a long way from those white officers in Moore's photograph, those agitated and frightened white men who pressed King against the counter, twisting his arm behind his back, arresting him for eternity in the objective space of that everlasting image. But I realize I'm also guilty. I've let my own subjective fear shape the way I define loitering. I've let my imagination carry me away, let my own context—home and family, children and dog, yard and garden—condition the meaning of the teenagers' nothingness, and I've let it color their lingering at the periphery of my space. The street is the line, I tell myself. It's a wide and fuzzy boundary between us. But it is a boundary.

One day a boy crossed the line. He approached the house. The kids were in the front yard. My friend met him at the driveway. I'd gone inside for a minute and came out to see her walking back toward the garage. She moved with purpose. I followed her. The boy waited at the end of the driveway.

"What's up?" I asked.

"He wants to borrow a soccer ball," my friend said as she smiled and walked past me, down the driveway and tossed him the ball. I felt my blood cool, retreating from full boil. There was no danger, no threat. There was nothing for me to fear.

"It's OK," she said.

The boy and his three friends, another boy and two girls, set up "goals" in the middle of the street made of wadded-up fast-food bags and wrappers. They played soccer on the asphalt for a while, darting out of the way when cars came. They were out there long enough for my kids and I to drift back inside. The boys flirted shamelessly with the girls and showed off with the ball. All of them laughed a lot. They seemed so happy. I watched them through the windows near the front door, listening to the sounds of their youth. They moved with ease and grace between the curbs, lingering in the in-between spaces with such sweet purpose.

IT BEGINS WITH A KNOCK AT THE DOOR

If you had spent enough time with me during the days and months shortly after our cross-country move from Rhode Island to Fresno, I would've probably told you about the helicopters overhead or about my new neighbor, Myrtle. She was eighty-three years old, had lived in her house for seventy-six years, and she had a boyfriend, Larry, who was eighty-nine. They were in love, full of life, and the kind of people you often refer to as *characters*—suggesting that they were part of some larger story you caught first in drops and glimpses and, if you were lucky, absorbed in deeper, more dangerous ways. Mostly I felt like a parasite, a sponge, watching and recording details, cataloguing them away, slowly constructing a narrative around my neighbors, waiting for my opportunity to tell it. Mostly I think I was jealous of them and the obvious love they shared.

Every now and then I got a true window into their lives.

And then I had to figure out how to see myself again in the reflection.

* * *

This is what I noticed: Larry came over every day around 4:00, parked his green Oldsmobile in front of Myrtle's house, and the two of them left shortly after for dinner—sometimes the Golden Chinese restaurant nearby, or maybe that new place Myrtle enjoyed, the Elephant Bar; but Larry really liked the riblets at Applebee's so that's where they usually dined. They came home before 6, drank cheap white wine, watched television, and then

Larry left around 9 or 10. Myrtle walked him to his car. This was their nightly ritual, their habit and predictable orbit.

I'm not actually sure what Myrtle did most of the day before Larry showed up. I watched out my window, but I didn't see much of her. She was a reluctant gardener, watering only when absolutely necessary and fussing unreasonably about her scraggly rose bushes. I suppose she watched television, maybe soap operas or talk shows, Fox News or sports. She must have had errands to run, friends to visit. She drove a Chevy Nova and regularly had to fend off offers to buy it. The car was in mint condition.

On the occasion that we saw each other in the yard, Myrtle would tell me she liked it when I played my drums in the garage and that she hated the honeysuckle that draped over our back fence (because it shaded her roses). I think she had a sister who lived nearby and a grandson who visited rarely. I knew she watched football on the weekends, baseball in the summer, and *Who Wants to Be a Millionaire?* whenever it was on. I heard the television trickling through open windows. Maybe she knitted or played bingo or parked herself in front of a slot machine at one of the casinos.

I didn't know everything about Myrtle—just enough to make me wonder, speculate, and imagine. Like all good ones, her character revealed itself in layers, giving the reader, the watcher, those cherished visions of something deeper, something unpredictable in her story.

To the outside observer, and to many of my friends and neighbors, my own life probably seemed highly suspicious, the kind of life that would make a neighbor skeptical if he happened to be watching me.

I wrote. I read. I taught a couple of classes a week, usually at night. I edited a literary magazine. I spent a good portion of my day at home wearing sweatpants and a black T-Shirt or hooded sweatshirt that read, "Trust me. I'm Normal," and staring at a computer screen or a stack of paper, a book or magazine. If you were lucky you might catch me puttering around the yard in basketball shorts and a pair of polystyrene gardening clogs. I kept my hair short so I didn't have to shower before leaving the house.

Once when I was out in the yard in the middle of the day, our neighbor from across the street, Jesse, came over to say hello. We exchanged pleasantries and chatted for a while. Then he looked at my baggy shorts and clogs and asked, "What do you *do*, anyway?"

I wanted to say, *I am a parasite, Jesse. I feed off of your life essence.* But this didn't seem appropriate.

"I teach at the University," I said; and when that didn't seem to register, I added, "I'm a Professor," as if this would somehow clarify things. My wife told me I should say I am a "writer," and she would often pipe up in these situations to say just that. But most people don't really think of that as a job.

"Is that like a full-time job?" Jesse asked.

"Yeah," I said. But I could tell he didn't really believe me. While it may be a lot of work, and at times quite difficult, I wouldn't call writing and teaching a job—or at least not in the traditional sense. I've had such jobs: painting houses, working excavation and construction, fixing toilets, sinks, refrigerators, disposals and dishwashers; and what I do now is quite different.

Jesse had just started working nights at the SC Johnson factory recently and would occasionally send one of his kids over with a scented candle, bottle of Windex, or box of Ziploc baggies, which I thought was very generous of him. These were the perks of his job. The perks of my job were time, space, freedom, and comfortable clothes—very similar, it just so happens, to the perks of early retirement.

What Jesse maybe didn't see was that, as a writer who looked retired, I was actually always working—in my head at least, often on several tasks at once. This is what a good parasite does; and I find that as I've aged, I've become a much more efficient parasite. I was already working on Jesse as soon as I met him. I was creating him as a character, imagining things about him and what goes on behind the doors of his house. I saw the blue glow of his television emanating from covered windows. I saw the odd knickknacks, the closet full of Ziploc baggies and bottles of Windex, the unmade beds, and the television's eternal glow. I saw the boys playing football in the street, his daughters sunbathing on the driveway in the hot sun, too young to tan. I saw them playing in an abandoned shopping cart. I saw shirtless Jesse, his longhaired brother, other men in white tank tops, most of them friendly and willing to engage with me in some lighthearted sports trash talk. I liked to tell Jesse that my yard was Celtic-green. He would laugh and hoisted a can of Busch Light and said, "My grass is Laker yellow!" I've never been in his house, relying instead on brief glimpses from my office window and our occasional across-the-street interaction.

I could understand why Jesse didn't recognize what I do as a job. I have trouble with it myself sometimes. Writing isn't really a job so much as it is a pathology, a life of the mind that—if you are extremely lucky--someone pays you to indulge. It is an identity, a uniform you put on and never take off. It is a lens more than a vocation. It is a way of seeing the world; and perhaps it is also a fence that separates you, insulates you, *and* protects you. I was beginning to worry that it isolated me from the everyday commerce of human life, the meat-and-potatoes emotional sustenance that keeps everyone else going. I was beginning to think it encouraged me to objectify everything and everyone, to see the world not as it is but as raw material for an essay.

More simply put, I worried that being a writer made me a bad neighbor and a bad person, perhaps even a bad husband and a bad father.

I told these stories about my neighbor, Jesse—this story you've just read—where he doesn't understand what I do for a living or how it counts as a job; and I would often include an aside about how Jesse liked to park his cars on the lawn despite an abundance of parking spaces on the street. I told this story in bars, at parties, and to my friends; and I didn't worry too much about how it made Jesse look as a character. I told this story because, in the end, it was a story about me and my guilt over not having a *real* job.

I needed Jesse's character to draw that conflict out in me. I needed to show it, let the reader feel it; because deep down I don't want to feel guilty for not having an 8-5 job, for not working with my hands (all things I've done before in my life), and for having one of those jobs my neighbors and my children don't even understand. Jesse had six children he mostly raised on his own. I could barely keep up with two and get my writing done. He worked hard and so did I; it just didn't look that way. I didn't want to feel guilty for being a parasite, living off the story possibilities in the world around him, and getting paid to do it—but I also couldn't deny my nature.

* * *

When I met Myrtle the first week we moved into our house, we stood in the yard talking. She pointed to Jesse's house and said, "They're Mexican. They make a lot of noise," then she pointed across the street and said, "They're black," as if that summed up the identity of our new neighbors. And as she said these things,

I felt myself slip slide away from the present moment and into my writer-mind where, as she was talking, I thought: *I'm going to write about this. I'm going to write about you saying these things right now that you're saying to me . . .*

I also wondered how she would define me.

This was happening a lot to me during those days—this constant essaying on identity. It was a kind of active disengagement or passive engagement. It happened with my wife and children, with my colleagues and my students. I was there but not there. I was often already taking an experience, filtering it, and crafting it into story, already cataloguing details, already imagining how it would go down on the page or how it might tumble around in my consciousness. And I think this made me a good writer. It was after all a pretty productive time in my writing life. But every now and then the story shifted and thrust an ending upon me that I didn't see coming, and, like a dithering slap to the face, forced me out of my writer-mind and into the present moment again.

One night as I sat at my computer working, a window opened up and a story about Myrtle fell right into my lap. It appeared as if I had conjured it up from the ether, inventing everything I'm about to tell you. But I didn't. It's all true and inherently dangerous, unpredictable, and strange.

It began like many stories, with a sound— a knock at the door, late at night.

I listened from the back room. My wife called to me, "Steve, come here. Myrtle needs your help. Larry fell in the bathtub."

I felt myself go into that separate place, felt a lens slide down over my eyes and my brain shift into the hyperaware writer-mind state. It was a strange and exhilarating feeling.

Myrtle met me at the door, and she was smiling but I could tell it was a forced smile. She fidgeted with her hands.

127

"Oh, gee whiz," she said, "I don't know what I'm going to do with him."

"What's up, Myrtle?"

"Oh, Larry fell in the bathtub. He was washing his hands and he said he lost his balance."

I tried to parse out the images that flooded my head and tamp down the speculation they ignited. *Washing his hands? In the tub?*

"Is he OK?" I asked, and then I heard something quietly but clearly—a fart. Myrtle *farted*.

"I think so. There's blood everywhere. I just can't lift him," She said.

Then she farted again. I tried not to laugh. This wasn't funny. This was serious business. I tried to focus on the man in the bathtub, the stuff people would believe. I imagined Larry naked, slumped in the tub, a horrific gash to the head. And I hoped it wasn't true.

"I'll give you a hand," I said and start following her across the lawn.

Larry was over 6 feet tall and weighed at least 250 pounds, maybe more—all torso teetering on spindly legs. My wife called his shape "spider body."

Myrtle mounted the porch steps ahead of me, stood beneath the yellow light, looked up teary-eyed. "Thank you so much," she said, and then she farted again.

This can't be happening to me, I said to myself, trying not to laugh but already recording details I would need later to prove that this did, indeed, happen to me—the details I would need to put this down on paper and shape it into some kind of story. And it is this detail—the farting—that, if I happen to be telling you this story, will make you laugh or wince and possibility doubt the truth of my tale. And if this should happen, then you are feeling exactly what I felt when it happened, and I've done my job as a writer.

When I came through Myrtle's green-carpeted living room into her bathroom, I saw the white corner of the tub smeared with blood. I moved quickly and found Larry reclined in the deep bathtub, his hands up on the sides as if he was floating in a warm bath. But he was not. The tub was dry. Larry wore a blue cotton leisure shirt, white Bermuda shorts, white athletic socks, and white tennis shoes. He was alive and conscious, but a little disoriented. I was just glad he wasn't naked or dead. Now I had to figure out how to get him out.

He couldn't pull himself up, just didn't have the arm strength. I draped his legs over the edge and worked his body around in the tub so that he was facing me instead of the wall. I stood in front of him, grabbed his arms, wedged my own feet against the side of the tub and pulled with all my weight and strength. It was like deadlifting a large sea mammal.

Larry couldn't really help and just sort of grunted and wiggled around a little, his elbow wound smearing blood across the yellow tile on the wall. I pulled as hard I've ever pulled and feel a twinge in my back. I think I was close to herniating a disc or busting a hole in my diaphragm. But I didn't stop. I kept tugging on his arms and when I lugged his body up to the edge of the tub, he worked his feet down to the floor and sat on the edge, still holding my hands. I re-set my grip, grabbing him by the upper arms and pulled him forward, into a standing position.

He teetered there in front of the tub, and I worked my way to his side while still holding him. He kept explaining that he'd just backed up too far after washing his hands. I held a hand to his back and kept him from flopping back in the tub. I felt him tipping, leaning over the chasm, and I worried. He's as top-heavy as a flightless bird. I looked down at the floor. There really wasn't much space between the sink and the tub. I could fall in there, I thought, especially if I'd had a few drinks. I've heard that 80% of deaths in the home are caused by falls in the bathroom. This could have been one of them, one of the statistics, one of the stories.

I helped Larry to a chair in the living room while Myrtle went to get a bandage for his bleeding elbow. He sat there for a moment and let me check his head for bruises but told me that he was fine; he just lost his balance.

"Can you tell me my name, Larry?" I asked, knowing that even in his most lucid state this could sometimes be a challenge.

"Steven Church," he said and pointed at me, snapping his soft fingers. This is how I knew he probably hadn't suffered a serious head wound or a stroke. He sat for a moment or two and then, as if to prove to me or to himself that he was all right, he stood up. I wanted to tell him to stay seated, but I couldn't stop him. He was up under his own power and he was talking to me about freestone peaches, when suddenly he tilted, swayed, and toppled over again. I tried to catch him, grabbing futilely at his arm, but it was no use. He crushed a wooden TV-table and dented a plaster wall with either his elbow or his head.

"I shouldn't have had that third glass of wine," Larry said as I help him up again and settled him back down into his chair, hoping he would stay this time, thinking that this story just got more and more bizarre.

"Wow, three glasses, huh?"

"I shouldn't have had three glasses of wine without eating dinner."

"You ate dinner!" Myrtle barked as she came in the room. "We had Chinese food." She dabbed at his wounds with a wet washcloth, peeled the backing off of a Band-Aid and pressed it to his elbow. She'd done this before. She raised a boy on her own, sent him off to the Major Leagues to play baseball for the Mets and the Phillies. Then she watched him die of cancer. Myrtle is tough. But tonight she was nervous and scared, embarrassed to have me there, embarrassed that she couldn't help Larry, embarrassed maybe that she couldn't stop farting. I could tell she wasn't herself. She kept apologizing and telling me, "I couldn't do a thing to help him."

"You know, I knew I shouldn't have had that third glass," Larry said again.

"He didn't break my crystal did he?" she joked as I picked up a glass from the floor. She was trying to act tough.

"No, but he splintered that table pretty good," I said.

"I'm going to divorce you," she teased him.

"But we're not even married!"

Let me explain. This is the backstory I often provide for my audience, a digression I like to take: Larry and Myrtle are not married, but they love each other. This much is clear to anyone who spends time around the two of them. Myrtle was a friend to Larry and his wife for 30 years. When Larry's wife died, Myrtle became a closer friend to Larry, and things between them have settled into a pleasant routine. He comes over every afternoon and spends most of the evening with her. Then Larry drives home to his empty house. Myrtle doesn't let him spend the night; and she is not interested in living in his house. This is just the way they do things.

If you met him Larry would tell you, if given a chance, repeatedly about his wife of 64 years. He'd tell you that he worked as an engineer for PG&E and that he was in the war. He'd offer you peaches from the trees in his yard. Nectarines too. He'd tell you about the pool in his yard and his great grandchildren who come to play. He might regularly forget your name and introduce himself nearly every time you see each other, "I'm Larry," he'd say again and again.

Sitting in that chair in Myrtle's house, he *was* able to summon my name, both first and last, from the fog. He recovered quickly it seemed from his topple into the tub. His speech was good and he was as lucid as ever. He was probably dehydrated, a little drunk and just feeling faint. But at Larry's age, that can be a lethal combination—at any age really.

In a move that I can only blame on my writer-mind, on the distance and disengagement of that psychic space that tends to overtake me in certain meaningful moments—I lifted my pant leg and showed Larry and Myrtle the scar on the inside of my right calf.

"See that?" I boasted. "I fell over a retaining wall and it had a piece of rebar sticking out of it. Ripped a big gash in my leg. Eighteen stitches."

I waited for a reaction.

I was trying to be sympathetic, trying to connect with Larry, but I think I ended up sounding ignorant, shallow, and immature. I didn't mention that I was also a little bit drunk when I fell off that wall. I kept that little nugget to myself. "It can happen to the best of us," I said. "I mean, I was in my twenties when I did this."

I want to smack myself in the head, make my character stop talking, hook him off the stage and give him better lines.

Larry looked up at me.

"See that?" he said, lifting his pants and pointing to his leg. A long scar ran from his knee almost all the way down to his ankle.

I didn't say a word. I just shut up and listened. I knew my cue.

"Got that in the war in the South Pacific. Torpedo hit our ship. I was in the infirmary. Woke up and heard them say something about having to amputate it and I said, 'No thanks. I'll make it through the war,' and I did. I made it through the war," he says, stroking the leg a little. "Damn thing's given me trouble ever since. I've had surgery on it a few times."

At that moment I felt another shift, another slide out of that writer-mind and back into the present moment, into reality. I was jerked back to being human again, fully engaged, and I began to see the spidery threads of this experience, radiating out to the past, the present, and the future. And I was trapped, caught up in the vibrating hum of these impossible moments, vacillating between story and reality.

Myrtle picked up the splintered table.

"He swam all night holding onto another sailor who couldn't swim," Myrtle said and walked toward the back of the house without looking at me.

"10:30 at night until about 5:30 in the morning when we were rescued," Larry said, and I was struck dumb, silent, flabbergasted at the courage and strength it would take to do a thing like that. I realized—dimly at first, then brighter—that this man before me, this wobbly old man, was probably one of the bravest people I'd ever meet, the kind of person who deserves a different sort of story than I could offer.

I left that night knowing that I had helped Myrtle and Larry, but that I had missed something too. I told the story to my wife, trying not to miss any details, practicing my delivery. Then I sat down at my desk, wondering what to do with the story I'd been given. I started from the beginning. I started with the knock at the door. I started with that sound and how it changes the world.

A knock at the door. A call for help . . . and as I began, I saw myself from my own writer-mind, saw myself as a character standing there in my neighbor's living room. This young father, a writer, a kid really. This punk. This jackass. He thought he knew a lot of things, thought himself wise beyond his years. He

133

thought he was funny because he didn't leave out the farting, because he couldn't help describing Larry as a *large sea mammal*. He thought he could see where the story was going from where it started. But this writer couldn't imagine what it was like to be Larry or Myrtle. He knew nothing of raising a son alone, a son who would become a Major League baseball player, or of losing that son to cancer. He knew nothing of war, of torpedoes, or of a love that lasts for sixty-four years and more, knew nothing of such loss. He knew nothing of these people as real people. He only imagined, speculated, predicted what couldn't be predicted about them as characters. He was a simple neighbor, a man who could lift heavy things. They needed his help not because he was wise or funny or good at storytelling, certainly not because they need his sympathy or jokes or essays, but because he was big enough to pull Larry out of a bathtub.

* * *

This is how the story ended: You know some of this already. The summer after we moved to Fresno, I took my pregnant wife and my 5-year-old son to live in Madrid, Spain for month. We spent most of the month in a state of constant anxiety, not knowing if our daughter would be a healthy baby or if she might have some genetic anomalies. It was possible, they told us, that she might have Down syndrome or another related disorder, but nobody really knew anything for sure. I'd been invited for a temporary gig, teaching other people how to write stories about the people in their lives—basically teaching them how to be highly efficient parasites. It seemed like a great opportunity, but I'm not sure I could have predicted how difficult it would be as well. My son had a wonderful time and still fondly remembers his visit to the Louvre in Paris, where at the Mona Lisa he was escorted past the security boundary by a guard so he could get an up-close look at the iconic painting. My wife mostly remembers feeling abandoned in a strange city as I went off to work three days a week or attended mandatory readings and events at night.

When we returned to Fresno, Larry's car was parked in front of Myrtle's house like always. The preschool nearby was still noisy with children. The house next door was still for sale. Jesse's car was still parked on the dirt-patch he called a lawn. The trains still wailed through town. I saw Larry's car and I wondered if his balance was back.

I remembered how a week before we left for Spain, Myrtle had called one night around 9:30. Larry had fallen in the tub again. When I got there, I found him the same spot, his elbow split open again. This time Myrtle had tried to get him out herself, and Larry's blood had spotted and smeared her blouse. She'd put a dining-room chair in the tub, which Larry had tried to use to pull himself up. It was stained with blood and clearly useless.

I surveyed the scene and said, "Myrtle, just call me right away next time, OK?" though I hoped there wouldn't be a next time.

"I know I should have called sooner," she said. "I just didn't want to bother you."

"It's no bother," I told her.

Larry and I performed the same lift and dance we'd performed before; but this time his pants were undone and he clutched at them with one hand while I helped him regain his balance. I helped him get them up and buckled his belt. As I left that night, Myrtle's eyes watered up when she thanked me, and she wrung her hands as she talked about all the trouble Larry had been having with balance. I could tell she was worried about us leaving for Spain.

"When are you leaving," she asked me again and again.

Now we were home again and Larry's car was still parked there past dinnertime. They always went out for dinner in Larry's car. Something didn't feel right.

I called to my wife from the living room. "Look," I said, pointing. "What?"

"Larry's car," I said. "It's still there."

"Maybe he's living with her now," she offered.

"I don't think so," I said. "Something's wrong."

As I was talking, I saw Myrtle emerge from the backyard, dragging a hose and sprinkler. "I'm going to talk to her," I said and made my way outside, across the grass.

She smiled when she saw me, but she looked tired. "You're back!" she cackled. "How was Spain?"

"It was great. Just amazing," I said. "But it's good to be home." I looked over at our house, back at Myrtle's, and then my eyes landed on Larry's car. Myrtle saw me looking, shifted a little on her feet and let out a sigh.

"He fell again," she said. "In the bathtub."

"Oh no," I said, "and I wasn't here to help." As my words came out, Myrtle nodded her head, almost involuntarily, like a reflex, physically acknowledging my absence.

First she tried the guy across the street, the widower with the cats, but he wasn't home. Then she tried one of her tenants in the apartment house, hoping one of the baseball players from City College was home. Nothing. Nobody around. Our house dark and empty. Finally she broke down, crossed the street, and asked Jesse for help. He came over with his burly sons, and they got Larry out of the tub again and into a chair.

Larry just sat there for a while until Jesse and his boys left and the spectacle was over. He was a little dizzy and confused, but he didn't want to go to any damn hospital. Myrtle thought he might have hit his head. She thought he should just stay there. But he wanted to go home.

"I tried to stop him," she says.

Larry made his way to the door and, "He seemed OK," Myrtle says. "He said he was fine."

He walked out on the porch. Myrtle held his elbow like she always does, but she couldn't hold him up as he teetered, stumbled and he went over, fell down the front steps, slammed into the metal railing and hit his head on the concrete. Myrtle called an ambulance immediately and they came and loaded him up and took Larry to the hospital. He was still there and only dimly aware of what had happened. He'd live but he'd never be the same. The next day his granddaughter would come and drive his car away and it would never again be parked in his spot by the curb. Two years from this moment Larry would die while I was away again for a summer teaching stint in Mexico. He'd gone downhill ever since that last fall.

"Oh god, Myrtle. I'm really sorry," I said, and I meant it.

She sort of nodded and shook her head, but she didn't speak. Her eyes—these small bright blue pearls—filled with tears, and she turned away.

"Well," she said, "I better get to watering."

"OK, bye," I said.

I turned away and walked back to our house. I didn't want the story to end this way. When I told it later to friends or family I often didn't get this far, never making it to the part where there is no easy resolution, or where the resolution seems all too predictable and sad. I'd stop with the first fall in the tub, the uncontrollable farting. People liked that. It was funny and awkward. Nobody wanted to hear about Larry falling down the stairs, confined to a bed, away from Myrtle. We all wanted to believe that everything was the same, believe that the story never changed and was always funny and weird and safe. We wanted to believe that love lasts forever because that's a nice story. We all enjoyed the luxury of humorous distance.

There was little I could do for Larry and Myrtle, but I wished I could make it up to them, help them, maybe change things so that Larry would be released from the hospital, allowed to drive again, and return to his life with Myrtle. I hated to admit it, but stories aren't that powerful. They can't change the fact that Larry would be bedridden, confined to his big empty house with a nursemaid tending to him, his body breaking down, putting up boundaries that would keep him away from his life with Myrtle forever. Though it would be two years before he finally passed away, he left Myrtle for good that night. And I wasn't there to help. I didn't like thinking about that, but it was true.

I wished I could do more than feed off my neighbor hosts. I wished I could give something back and be more symbiotic. If I tell their story enough times, I like to think I can go back and be present through the retelling, be that good neighbor or friend in the moment who helps unselfishly without searching for the story possibilities, the kind of neighbor who is present, engaged, humble and simply helpful. This seems like the least I can do, not just for my neighbors but also for my own family, for my children.

I like to imagine how I might have sat Larry down and listened quietly as he talked. Perhaps I would've asked about his injury or the torpedo, his time in the water, swimming all night, clutching that other sailor, keeping another man alive.

Were the sharks circling? I'd have asked this time. *Tell me about the sharks.*

Maybe he would've talked to me, told me his own stories that could push this one out of my head. Maybe my presence would've been enough to convince Larry to linger a while, to rest in the chair, or allow me to help him down the steps and into his Buick. I like to imagine myself the next day hauling my toolbox across the lawn, installing safety bars and handrails in Myrtle's bathroom because I know how to do that kind of work, too. And I can just see Myrtle fussing over the mess it made on her carpet. I like to picture myself watching from my front porch as Larry and Myrtle drive off again and again, night after night, destined for a routine riblet dinner, this scene of love looping on eternally; but I had no say over this scene or the larger story, no agency through imagination, because it was all impossibly, uncontrollably, and tragically true.

PLAYLIST FOR FINISHING A BOOK

Track 1: "For Whom the Bell Tolls,"[1] Metallica, *Ride the Lightning*

After I dropped my daughter with Teacher Xue at the campus day care, I had to get home fast, get in front of the screen and get "some work done." I had a manuscript due to a publisher in a couple of months. The book I was trying to finish, a long-suffered

---

1   [10] The book, *The Day After The Day After: My Atomic Angst* is about the personal, historical, and cultural legacy of apocalypse as seen through the lens of the TV melodrama, *The Day After*, a movie set and filmed in my hometown, Lawrence, Kansas. I wrote most of it, though, in Fresno. In my acknowledgements I specifically thank Metallica (as if they need it) for their first two albums and describe my editing and revision process as a caffeine-and-adrenaline-fueled mosh pit," and while that may have been a bit of an exaggeration, it wasn't much of one—at least in terms of the musical soundtrack to much of the process. I spent a good portion of any given day listening to metal, thinking about the end of the world and watching clips from movies like *The Day After* or *Red Dawn*. I wasn't perhaps in the best place psychologically. But that didn't change my responsibilities. At that time my daughter was in daycare four days a week, four hours a day, and, with drop-off and pick-up, I had about twelve hours a week of time alone, at home with no distractions, to work on revisions of the book. So I'd sit down in front of my computer and crank up the volume on Metallica and Judas Priest, Iron Maiden, Dio, Megadeath and more until the blinds in my office rattled from the noise and I'd attack my manuscript, tearing into it in a metal-fueled slam dance of destruction and creation. When it was working, the two forces operated together to make something new or at least produce a sentence I could appreciate. The truth was that a well-rendered sentence had the effect for me of ordering the day and making sense of a chaotic world. When the process didn't work there was just rambling post-apocalyptic devastation and a festering gut-bomb in my stomach from drinking too much coffee and listening to too much metal.

manuscript built up over ten years or more, began as one long messy essay, a "messay" that haunted me at times with shifting forms and foci, and a book that I'd many times left for dead. Some days it helped to think of myself as a mad scientist tinkering with his monster, because I knew I'd have to rebuild the book like Frankenstein built his beast or like Oscar Goldman re-jiggered his wounded astronaut in *The Six-Million Dollar Man*, making it bigger, stronger, smarter, and faster. And each morning as I drove away from my daughter's school and gathered myself for the work ahead, I'd often hear the bells tolling, the end already approaching, Metallica reminding me that I'd soon have to send my creation off into the forest to fight the robotic Bigfoot, or into the square to face the angry villagers. But before that, I'd have to pick my daughter up from daycare, feed her lunch, and try to get her to take a nap. These things didn't change. They were as predictable as the sun and helicopters in Fresno, the forsaken city.

Track 2: "Seek and Destroy, "[2] Metallica from *Kill 'Em All*

The 1986 sci-fi movie classic, *Highlander*, has seemingly little to do with Metallica's 1983 metal classic, "Seek and Destroy," especially since the movie soundtrack was done by the prog-rock giant, *Queen*; so it's difficult for me to explain exactly how the

---

2   At around the same time I was trying to finish *The Day After the Day After* and spending a lot of time with my baby daughter, I read a story about the use of music to torture detainees in Guantanamo, Abu Ghraib, and other US detention facilities in, for example, Iraq and Afghanistan. It had the effect of shifting my understanding of the world in strange ways. It burrowed under my skin. The article included a "top ten" list of bands and songs, and I was disheartened but not surprised to find many of my favorite bands on that list. I've since been unable to find the original article, but a quick online search will take you to several stories and lists of top torture songs. Metallica, of course, makes most of the lists, often with perhaps their most radio friendly hit, "Enter Sandman," from *The Black Album*, a song that is, in my opinion, perhaps the catchiest and silliest song the band has ever recorded. It is a song about death featuring an almost sing-song chorus based a children's nursery rhyme and alluding to the children's classic *Peter Pan* (a stylistic choice which, though similar, I would argue is markedly different from the creepy Oompa-Loompa-esque chanting in "Frayed Ends of Sanity" on their previous album *And Justice for All*). If you try, you can sing most of "Enter Sandman" like a nursery rhyme. It's metal for children. And apparently for torturers. But I still can't fathom what it would be like to listen to it constantly, to have to tune it out somehow if you wanted to sleep. Sergeant Mark Hadsell told *Newsweek* magazine: "These people haven't heard heavy metal before. They can't take it. If you play it for 24 hours, your brain and body functions start to slide, your train of thought slows down and your will is broken. That's when we come in and talk to them." Try it. Try to listen to the song and hear the melody of, "Exit light. Enter night. Take my hand. Off to never never land," but then imagine it played over and over and over again, all night long. Though it pains me to admit this here on the page, James Hetfield, lead singer of Metallica has said about his music being used to torture human beings, "We've been punishing our parents, our wives, our loved ones with this music for ever. Why should the Iraqis be any different?" (The Guardian, June 18, 2008). And here is a truth that I suppose many of us must face some day: occasionally our heroes of art and music disappoint us deeply.

two 80s masterpieces were connected in my head. But somehow it all made sense to me. In *Highlander*, Sean Connery plays the benevolent, stylish and immortal Spanish swordsman, Juan Sanchez Villa-Lobos Ramirez who takes Christopher Lambert's equally immortal and exiled character, Connor MacLeod under his tutorial wing after McLeod is banished from his Scottish clan for being "in league with Lucifer." The two are part of an elite and dying breed of immortals being hunted down by The Kurgan, a massive rampaging Cossack played by Clancy Brown who is hell-bent on becoming the last immortal standing so that he alone might experience the ultimate "quickening", known as "The Prize," the final gift that would allow an immortal to be both mortal and fertile.

In one memorable scene, The Kurgan stalks into a church (holy ground—and the only safe zone for Immortals) for a meeting with MacLeod. Punked out in leather and zippers, he strolls down the aisles, smacking the pews and frightening the people bent in prayer. As he's leaving, he punches his fists into the air and lets out a raspy growl:

"It's better to burn out than to fade away!"

This scene is important for me because in those anxious days, with a book deadline approaching, I only had so much time before I had to pick my daughter up from daycare and I had a lot of revision left to do, a lot of hard choices; and some days at it helped to write to a soundtrack, to imagine I was the immortal Kurgan, my neck stitched up with safety pins, and I was coming after my book, fueled not by Queen but by Metallica's first album *Kill Em All*.

I wasn't writing at this point, wasn't creating. I was *searching*, *searching* to *seek and destroy* the weak sentence, *burning* for revision, *burning* because some of those paragraphs and sentences refused to die, and because it wasn't enough to just kill my darlings. Some days I had to slaughter them. Sometimes I gathered up the dead and collected them in a pile on my hard drive. Other times I let them go into the trash, gone for good, never to return. I'd do this for hours until I realized that my ears were ringing, my butt was starting to sweat in my chair, and I needed to take a break, slip on my polystyrene gardening clogs, and get outside in the yard, away from my desk. I needed to slow down, breathe, and water the giant bird of paradise, a plant that never did produce the promised bloom, no matter how much I nurtured it. I'd stand out there for a while watching the way the water beaded up and rolled off the fat leaves, down the stalks into the roots; I waited foolishly for a bird flower. And I realize now that in these moments between revisions, I was just trying to keep something, *anything* alive.

"Callin' Out," Lyrics Born[3] from *Later That Day*

Some days during the revision process I needed to live in a different kind of sound. My desk would begin to feel like the sort of psychic space that confined and bottled me up, a static space filled with metal noise and anxious energy, and I needed to change the vibe and mood of the day. Sometimes it was too much, and I just had to move, had to get away from the desk and dance happy-like in the kitchen while my daughter ate lunch in her high chair. I'd crank up "Callin' Out" when I needed a pep talk, a pick-me-up, and a

---

3   Lyrics Born, AKA Tsutomu "Tom" Shimura, is a Bay Area rapper and producer and the son of Japanese author, Takao Shimura. Like most rappers, Shimura samples heavily from other music, appropriating the art of others to create something new and different. Shimura is very good at what he does. Thankfully he wasn't included on the infamous list of torture music, perhaps because his lyrics are too esoteric, too affirming or intelligent and impossible to pigeonhole; but other rap and hip-hop music *was* favored by torturers and inflicted on prisoners. It wasn't all metal all the time. And it makes sense that the musical taste of torturers would reflect the diversity of the people doing the torturing and, to some extent, of American culture writ large. It also makes sense, cruelly and ironically, that hip-hop music, an art form defined by appropriation, would in turn be appropriated. The difference is that the only thing the torturers are creating through their appropriation is pain, suffering, and true terror. There is no art in the terror we've created in the name of preventing terror. On some level it also doesn't really matter what kind of music is used. Torturers love everyone from Elvis to Insane Clown Posse. Suzanne Cusick, a music professor at New York University, has interviewed a number of former detainees about their experiences. Played at a certain volume, Cusick said, the music "simply prevents people from thinking." Binyam Mohamed, a British resident held in Guantánamo Bay said that the constant loud music made him feel that he was losing his sanity . . . while being hung up and deprived of sleep, "there was loud music. [Eminem's] Slim Shady and Dr. Dre for 20 days ... plenty lost their minds. I could hear people knocking their heads against the walls and the doors, screaming their heads off."

rhythmic reminder that I didn't have to wiggle myself into box all day, that deadlines were not my enemy. My daughter couldn't see the date looming on the calendar as she chucked peas on the floor and banged her yogurt covered spoon like it was a judge's gavel. She just wanted a show. She wanted to see me shaking my ass in the kitchen, smacking my butt to the beat. She loved to watch me dance and often giggled appreciatively from her chair like the "principessa" her Opah calls her. Other times she stood in the doorway, her big brown eyes staring from beneath her blonde bangs and her lip curling into a smile because I look cartoon silly when I dance, and her legs would bend in mimicry, her little butt bouncing right along with mine.

"You've Got Another Thing Comin'," Judas Priest[4] from *Best of Judas Priest: Living After Midnight*

Soon enough I began to realize that my Kurgan-inspired mosh pit approach to writing and revising was bleeding over a bit into

---

4   There's something about having a baby daughter, spending so much time with her, that amplifies my indignation with the injustices of the world. I was supposed to be finishing the book, but I seemed to keep stumbling down these rabbit holes of research, these side trips into the meaning of music as both therapy and torture. I chased sound and morality, noise and transcendence, ears and music, not knowing it would lead to another book. What did it mean, really, that the songs I nostalgically love, songs that make me happy, were used by representatives of my country to destroy psychologically other human beings? Sometimes it was hard to imagine raising a child in a world where such incongruities existed, a world where art can be appropriated so easily and so unethically. I was trying to understand with my own book the relationship between art and ethics (a dilemma that nonfiction writers carry around like Quasimodo's hump), and increasingly believing that art, while perhaps created in one, doesn't exist in a vacuum once it is given to an audience. Once you turn art loose into the world there's no controlling how people interact with it, appropriate, or abuse it. The musicians themselves on the list also struggle mightily with the ways their work has been appropriated, perhaps even corrupted, forever. Tom Morello, famous now for his rebuke of VP candidate Paul Ryan's professed love for Morello's music and his band Rage Against the Machine was equally outraged when he discovered that some of his songs were also on an expanded list of those used in detention facilities. Morello and other musicians demanded that the full list of songs be released and that the practice stop immediately. Quoted in *The Guardian* on Dec. 10, 2008, Musician David Gray, also on the list, said, "What we're talking about here is people in a darkened room, physically inhibited by handcuffs, bags over their heads and music blaring at them. That is nothing but torture. It doesn't matter what the music is. It could be Tchaikovsky's finest or it could be Barney the Dinosaur. It really doesn't matter, it's going to drive you completely nuts."

my teaching—and perhaps not in ways that were particularly healthy. I'd created a "pre-workshop" playlist (a smaller subset of my "Metallicious" playlist) that I listened to while driving to class. It included mostly old Metallica ("Jump in the Fire," "For Whom the Bell Tolls," and "Seek and Destroy"), along with "Looks that Kill" by Mötley Crüe, "Run To the Hills" by Iron Maiden, "Holy Diver" by Dio, Danzig's "Mother," and the gut-rumbling, bowel-rattling full-body experience of Judas Priest's "You've Got Another Thing Comin'," a song that, when I played it loud, made pens and mugs, the rearview mirrors, everything in my car, vibrate and rattle. It was a song I liked to pretend was the soundtrack to my walk, my strut, my approach to leading a writing workshop; even if the truth is that most days it wasn't a strut at all but a bluesy confused stomp across a dusky parking lot toward the Family and Food Sciences Building where my class met. Some days this stomp led straight into a brawling, messy workshop. I paced around the floor, hands all over my face and head, nervously tugging at my ears, kicking the legs of the table on my anxious back and forth; and I'm sure the students were watching me, wondering if I was OK, if I was even paying attention. Or if I was thinking about the next morning at 5:00 a.m. and how I already knew I'd be sitting at my computer, staring through the faux-wood slats of our window blinds, and that if I was lucky I might be alone for a few moments as I tried cranking up my own engine, tried to get ready to write. Or, I was thinking about how my daughter would inevitably toddle out from her room, up early like her father, reminding me that I had another thing coming if I thought I was going to do anything besides hold her, maybe read her some books, or, after her mom left for work, turn up the music and dance again in the kitchen just to make her laugh.

"Keep Me," The Black Keys from *Rubber Factory*

After my daughter was born, my office moved from the bedroom at the back of the house to the breakfast nook set off the kitchen, with no door to separate me from the daily commerce of family life. The simple loss of a door meant the loss of a boundary between my work as a writer and my work as a father. Most of what I do as a teacher and writer is done at home, a place where all of my roles collide and overlap in a confusing, boundary-less existence. It sounds crazy but some days I envied the button-up life of an office drone or, more acutely, the predictable defined life I lived as a maintenance man, housepainter, or a construction worker. But I always reminded myself that such jobs provided boundaries, but they were also the sorts of boundaries that precluded the kind of relationship I wanted with my children. I wanted to wipe butts and cook and drive them to school. I wanted to be there early in the mornings like my mom was there for me, and I also wanted to be the dad who did fun things on the weekends. I wanted to be the dad who makes dioramas from stuff we find on the street. I still love being the only father at little-girl birthday parties on Saturdays and classroom parties on Fridays; I love being the one who doesn't always fit in with the wealthier mommies but who is perfectly happy to watch his daughter have fun swimming and prancing, bossing and pushing, asserting herself as a person. And this Black Keys tune, "Keep Me" was the song that my daughter and I danced to the most in the kitchen, the one I seemed to play over and over again, never growing tired of Dan Auerbach's voice. This is the one song to which my daughter would stand before me, arms up, demanding to dance. She'd grab my hand and hold one arm out in the pose of a waltz as the two of us dipped and swung and glided around the tiny kitchen; and the song began to feel like a lullaby of sorts, a promise I made each time to keep her soul away from harm.[5]

---

5   I have a terrible singing voice. Can't hold a note, can't carry a tune. But I still sang to my daughter every night as I rocked her to sleep and gave her a bottle. Mostly it was the classic stuff. Mary and her lamb, twinkle-twinkle, and maybe a few lines from the gospel and bluegrass classic, "Go to Sleep My Little Baby," combined with other lines that I just made up to go with the lilting tune. I never sang any metal or rap music, never broke into some lines from Judas Priest or Danzig, and I didn't soothe her with the sounds of "Enter Sandman." Mostly she didn't care for the noise of my music, but it's also just not terribly appropriate for a sleepy toddler. If you search, though, you can find an album of bluegrass covers of Metallica, a slightly softened and oddly appropriate take on many of their classic songs that even a child could love. More searching will lead you to an album called *Rockabye Baby: Lullaby Renditions of AC/DC*, another favorite band of mine, and of torturers. This album, though, is apparently intended to help your child drift peacefully off into dreamland, or at least help you relive your adolescence as you put them to bed. To achieve this, the list of songs includes the fan favorites, "Hells Bells," and "Back in Black," as well as a lullaby rendition of "Dirty Deeds Done Dirt Cheap," the persona song narrated from the point of view of a hired killer who offers his services at a discounted rate just in case, "you're havin' trouble with the high school head," or, "If ya got a lady and ya want her gone, but you ain't got the guts."

"Roamin' Around,"[6] The Supersuckers from *Must Have Been Live*

And sometimes in the midst of all that angst and energy, all that aggressive writing and revision, I understood that, at times, writing essays and nonfiction need to be more like a dance or a walk around the block, roaming around with no point, no purpose, a journey that finds its terminus where it ends; and I had to recognize sometimes my best ideas came early in the morning, out walking the dog or walking with my daughter, the two of us

---

6   This song comes from the Supersucker's live country album, "Must've Been High," a classic alt-country album by a fairly hardcore alt-punk rock band. The recording was, at the time, one of the only country albums I owned. Country music seemed conspicuously absent from the torture list, perhaps because it's too slow, too easy, or sad, or close to home. I'd grown up with the Oak Ridge Boys and John Denver, a little bit of Johnny Cash, Willie Nelson, Kenny Rogers, and Merle Haggard but it wasn't until I got older and closer to finishing the book that I began drifting away from mostly metal back into the blues and country music. And my daughter was just a baby when I rekindled my appreciation for Waylon Jennings, a man who'd been one decision away from dying in the plane with the Big Bopper and Ritchie Valens. Jennings, also the former lead guitarist for Hank Williams, is someone I like for his lack of polish, for his faults and failings. Though he never achieved the commercial and critical success of his "outlaw" compatriots, Cash and Nelson, Waylon would carve out a deep place in my heart, thanks initially to his role as the balladeer on the 80s TV show, *The Dukes of Hazzard*, and more recently, because he would end up teaching my daughter how to spell one of her first and favorite words. His song, "Waymore's Blues," a song that Shel Silverstein once called an, "American folk classic," contains the line, "If you wanna get the rabbit out the l-o-g, you gotta make a commotion like a d-o-g," and was played on heavy rotation for a while in our house and in my car. We'd be driving and my daughter would bark, "Daddy, I want Waylon," and the two of us would sing along, me trying to mimic Waylon's laconic bass-toned voice and her singing, "d-o-g" on cue, smiling and laughing and demanding that I play it again and again. She never got tired of it. Sometimes I did, and I'd try to get her to sing along with me to other Waylon songs, but she always came back to, "Daddy, I want the d-o-g song."

listening to the soft hum of traffic in the distance, gazing silently from sidewalks into neighborhood windows, trying to imagine all the details of the lives inside, trying to see what they were eating or watching on TV at 6:00 a.m., trying to see how other families acted their parts.

"Going Home, "[7] Dan Auerbach from *Keep it Hid*

At some point I knew that in order to finish the book I'd have to go home, back to Kansas, back to where I was born. So I gathered myself and called Dad. I told him I was coming home for Father's Day, his birthday in 2007, and that I was coming home to see the apocalypse. The plan was to visit *his* hometown, Greensburg, Kansas, where just six weeks earlier an F5 tornado on May 4 had destroyed 95% of the town, including the home where my grandparents' had lived for sixty years, the same house where my father grew up, a house I visited regularly in the summers and for holidays, a house that had grown like a nautilus shell, adding

---

7   Our home is Fresno, California. I can say that now. It's only taken seven years to get to this point. My daughter was born here and has never lived anywhere else, never lived anywhere besides a world at war, anywhere besides a country that tortures. Our son may have lived in six houses and three states in the first four years of his life, but his sister's roots are deep in this place, this San Joaquin valley of heat and fruit, a landscape of great contradiction. It's a desperate place shaped by poverty and dislocation, but it is also a place of quiet beauty, of bounty, and art. It's a place of family and friends. And if there's one early image or memory of those first years in Fresno that is fixed in my mind, it would be a memory of our mornings together, just before dawn, sitting at my writing desk, reading the sports news online and listening to, or trying to ignore, news reports about war and torture, sitting silently, taking a break from the book, when I'd hear my daughter tumble out of bed and shuffle into the kitchen. I knew the sound of her heavy-heeled approach by heart, knew she was there before I ever turned around. Ever the early riser, she didn't want to miss anything. The nighttime police helicopters would have roosted for the day, sleeping off their spins, and the sun would've just barely begun to pink the sky, seeping in through the slats in the blinds. She'd stand there for a second in the half-light of the kitchen, naked but for her sagging diaper, hair askew, rubbing sleep crumbs from her eyes. Then she'd toddle over and climb up into my lap, carrying the warmth of sleep with her and pressing it into my body. She'd stay there until we felt like one breathing being, warm and awake and alive together for another day.

on chambers as the family grew. The twister had been on the ground for nearly a half hour, churning through the town, and all I can imagine is the noise, the terrible freight-train rumble of the storm. I knew I was coming home to see a pile of rubble, but I wanted to touch the apocalypse more directly. The wind had severely battered my Aunt Judy's large house on the northwest side of town as she huddled in the basement. Because it hadn't been in the direct path the house survived but was barely standing, lilting to one side. We were going to help her clean up a bit, to sift through the glass and debris, searching for sentimental items. In the pictures I'd found online, I saw piles of brick and wood spread across a grid of empty streets that didn't look at all like the streets I remembered. I told Dad I was coming home because I needed to see it in person, to feel the ideas that had been bouncing around in my head and needed to ground them in something real. He listened and promised to take me all the way back. I was going home for my father's birthday, going home to find the end. But I was also going back to reconnect with what it means to be a father, and with the idea of home. I wanted to touch a tangible disaster and find the end of a book; but somehow I knew, even as my flight lifted off from Fresno and cleared the Sierras, leaving my son and my daughter in the distance, that I might not find it in Kansas or California or any destination I can map on my own.

NOTES ON PROCESS AND SOURCES

The last few years I've been thinking more often about sound as a source for material and for form in an essay. This book is largely a product of that thinking. Given that many of our standard analogies for form in an essay (line, arc, braid, spider web, collage) arise from a visual medium and depend on graphic representations for their significance, I've become interested in how sound, often the forgotten sense in writing, can work as a kind of model for form and movement in an essay—all of which comes off as more esoteric than I initially intended. I started out trying to write essays (and a book now) that include sensory details of sound, are about sound in some way, but that also included work that moves by echolocation, by bouncing ideas or thematic "waves" off of pings in the distance, using sound to navigate ground that is perhaps dark and hidden beneath the surface. I wanted to think about how this subject, sense, and form might help me to mapping personally uncharted emotional and intellectual territory. "Ultrasonic" was perhaps the first successful attempt at this—a piece that, as it took shape, began to expand and grow until I was seeing and hearing everything through the filter of sound or noise, until I found myself paying attention to the world around me in ways I hadn't before and in ways that began to show up on the page. And I suppose this is one of the things I love most about essays—not just the exploration and discovery (which is immensely satisfying by itself) but the sense that essaying can somehow make the world seem full of wonder, that writing (in the most hyperbolic expression of this) can make you a better person, or at least more aware of the world around you everyday.

Auscultation:

This essay began with form. Or at least I think it did. Or it began with research into the history of stethoscopes, the word, "auscultation." So many of these essays take etymologies as a starting or pivot point. I knew the essay was in some way about using sound to see beneath the surface; and, pretty quickly, as I started writing about stethoscopes and auscultation, I knew the final version would have four parts, or four "chambers." And it was this word, this idea of *chambers* beneath the surface that led me back to the two stories of trapped miners—form leading to content and meaning. Once I began to accumulate the pieces of the essay, I wanted to try and construct movement, tension, and depth without relying too much on traditional narrative structure. I wanted a sound or an idea, an echo of a larger theme, to be the thing that carries the reader from one section to the next, not (just) the dramatic tension of "what's going to happen next?" I guess I also wanted to create the illusion of free-form improvisation while still keeping everything within the digressive logic and thematic constraints of what I think of as a fairly traditional meditative essay. I'm more interested in principled digression or juxtaposition than simple fragmentation for the sake of fragmentation. I want the moves, if not entirely clear at first, to feel nonetheless like the product of intentional thought and reflection, rather than the by-product of accidental (or at least mysterious) arrangement. If the moves in the essay don't make obvious *sense* at first, I wanted them to at least *sound* right.

Ultrasonic:

The original intent of this essay was to write about racquetball. That's all. I'd been playing racquetball alone, in the mornings, and found that I loved this time to myself, perhaps disproportionately, obsessively, in ways that I couldn't fully articulate. So I tried to write about how much I enjoyed chasing a little blue ball around a court—and, more specifically, why I enjoyed it most when I was alone.

The first paragraph about the noise of racquetball was the first paragraph I wrote. I was trying to capture the soundscape of the game. That this remains the first paragraph in the final draft is rare for me. Often the first thing I write is buried deep in a piece or excised completely—created only as a spark and fuel to the essay's engine and then quickly burned up. This time, I wrote that paragraph and sat staring at it. Then I put it away for a while. At that point, there wasn't really anything about transcendence or our unborn baby. There were just descriptions of the blue ball and the noise.

When I came back to the essay, when I couldn't ignore the way it had begun to shape my thinking, I decided that every time I sat down to write I would guide my digressions or tangents in some ways by the constraints, "blue" and "noise," "blue noise," or "sound," trusting that the literal and metaphorical meanings of these things, as well as the connections between sound and transcendence would arise from the details. If I went off on a tangent, I just inserted a page break, giving the tangent it's own space to breathe, and kept going.

It was a very deliberate thinking assignment, a kind of mapped digression into the thicket of consciousness, an associative journey and a challenge not just in form but also in style and voice. I've come to think of *Ultrasonic* as the first in a series of what I call "constraint" essays, where I give myself a somewhat artificial form and system of limits. It was a way to harness my mind's tendency to ramble and a kind of test to see how far I could stretch within these constraints. I wanted to rely less on the "I" on the page at times and push myself to try on a different sort of narrative costume and role—that of the collector or curator who gathers scraps, bits of information, voices and images, and then assembles patterns of meaning on the page.

All of a Dither:

This essay began with one sentence. I discovered it while doing research for "Ultrasonic." Somewhere on the Internet I found a page outlining the different shades of noise and I followed a path of links down the rabbit hole into a wonderland of sound engineering. We all know about white noise, but I never realized there were such things as black noise, orange noise, pink noise, and blue noise. The sentence that started it all, a quote from a textbook on sound engineering, read, "Blue noise makes a good dither," and I realized that I loved this sentence deeply and irrationally. I loved it because it was a puzzle. I had no idea what "blue noise" was or what "dither" really meant, even if I'd heard the word before. So I turned to my enormous leather-bound edition of the Webster's Unabridged Third New International Dictionary, and looked up "dither." Everything in the first section of the essay in italics is taken verbatim from the Webster's entry there. The reference to Wallace Stevens comes from his poem "Variations on a Summer Day" which includes the lines, "Words add to the senses. The words for the dazzle / Of mica, the dithering of grass." Much of the initial material here was written as a kind of free-writing self-assignment centered on the constraints of "blue" and "noise." But at some point an essay began to appear from the larger surrounding material, sort of like one of those 3-D posters that were popular for a while where you have to stare at them for a long time, letting your eyes drift from the center, looking through the image, and suddenly a dinosaur or a fighter jet appears. The essay began to be what I call "sticky," when the piece took on its own forward momentum, gathering up bits of personal experience and research as it progressed, until I begin to see everything through the lens of the essay. With "All of a Dither," I became interested in the physicality and language of sound; and at some point I began to think of children as "dithers," these tiny little noisy engines of blue noise and chaos that help rattle our gauges and keep us cranking, and from there the essay took me back to my own birth and, as often happens, into pop culture touchstones like Arthur Fonzarelli from the hit TV sit-com *Happy Days* and other practitioners of "ape mechanics."

Seven Fathoms Down:

This one began at a bar with one word. In response to something I can't recall, I used the phrase, "Oh, that just warms my cockles," and a friend looked at me funny, questioning the phrase, wondering what the word "cockles" really means. So we looked it up, right there on our phones and found that a cockle was a thing, a shellfish, a heart-shaped valve, and *also* a sound. It was shape and sound, object and wave. I suppose I'd already become interested in the physicality of sound and the synesthetic blur of language that accompanies it, so it didn't take much to get lost in the language. The essay began simply as an exploration of the words, "sounding," "fathom," and "cockles," but then (as essays often do) took me off into other places, back home to Kansas and finally to a subject I'd written about before, one I thought I'd left behind. And though may seem like bullshit, like some overly writerly crap I invented, I can honestly say I did not expect the essay to go there, did not see the drowning coming on the page. I discovered the subject of the essay by writing my way into it. For me this is yet further confirmation that there is something productive for me in these constrained essays I've been writing, something that allows me a new way of seeing old experiences.

Bird Watching in Fresno:

Do you live in a place where police helicopters are omnipresent? If so, perhaps you understand the origins of this essay. For me, a Kansas kid who'd grown up amidst the summer cacophony of cicadas and apocalyptic storms, wind and thunder and lightning, I thought I'd heard haunting noise. But something about the drone and hum, the chop and whir of the helicopters began to grate on me. I hated the helicopters' noise because it seemed like a warning or a taunt. I was sure we'd made a horrible mistake moving to this place, this poverty-stricken, drunken, and polluted place patrolled by helicopter gunships (not really), a city I've since grown to love in the way one loves one's own scars. It's ugly, but it's part of me now, like a new tougher skin. At the time, I just wanted the helicopters to go away. I wanted my daughter to sleep. I didn't want to feel like I was being watched. And I wanted to sit quietly in the dark of my backyard, listening to the trains or the faint hum of the freeway, even the hum of the neighbor's halogen security light, anything but that helicopter. I'm not sure how the essay ended up making that turn back to my adolescence, my own mix of fear and fascination with uncovered windows in the night. I really did occasionally imagine that I was being watched and flip the bird to whoever might be out there. It is a silly thing. Or maybe there is something else behind it, something I can only approach through such an essay and from the distance of thirty years.

Crown and Shoulder:

I wanted to write about a series of injuries to my head and my shoulder but I couldn't really figure out a way to do it that would be remotely interesting to anyone but myself. Some of the sections I'd written out before and abandoned in the scrap heap of my computer hard drive. But when I decided to explore within the constraints of "crown," and "shoulder," I found that the essay opened up and began to gather up the different scraps of story and language, taking on momentum that carried me into all sorts of unexpected territory. As with the "Seven Fathoms Down" essay, this is one where the subject, the final emotional turn, revealed itself to me only after writing my way into the midst of it without really knowing where I was headed. I did not expect to again be grappling with my brother's death. I figured I'd written about it enough. But the more I wrote, the more I explored the possibilities hidden within the constraints, the more obvious it became that I was circling around the fact that my brother had died on the shoulder of a street when his car hit a tree and he suffered a traumatic head injury. In retrospect it seems obvious—crown, shoulder, brother--but at the time it truly felt like a surprise, as if I'd navigated via echolocation once again into the dark territory of grief.

Lag Time:

This essay was originally part of the longer essay, "Ultrasonic," but I felt that subject matter-wise it was such a departure from the rest of the essay that I couldn't use it in that piece. So I cut it. And I kept it. Because I keep everything. I have huge files of drafts with many essays going through seven different versions or more. At some point I went back to look at this scrap, thinking there might be something that I could send to *Brevity*, a magazine I've admired for a long time but never had anything short enough to send. I wanted to talk about my father's lesson on "lag time" and lightning, but as with many of these pieces, I didn't expect that it would dredge up my brother's death. Yet there it was on the page, humming beneath the surface of so many things I've written. It didn't fit in the "Ultrasonic" essay but seemed to have its own life and shape, and it ultimately provided a companion to the previous "Crown and Shoulder" essay, perhaps another new way of looking at an old subject.

The King's Last Game:
The original intent was to write about racquetball. But then I stumbled across the double whammy of all racquetball-related trivia. Not only did Elvis Presley love racquetball enough to have a court built at Graceland, but he also played a game of racquetball on the night he died. It was, in fact, one of the last things he did before he died. Though "Ultrasonic" started with racquetball, it quickly digressed and branched out into other territory. This essay allowed me to return to some of the other things I love about the game while also exploring the connection between Elvis Presley, rock and roll, my father and racquetball. The essay helps introduce music as a source of material for the book, a thread that gets picked up and complicated in the last essay. This is also one of the few essays in the book where I rely on purely imagined scenes, fictionalized accounts of listening to Elvis play racquetball or of playing with him, and some of this is because I already think of Elvis as a kind of vessel for our hopes and dreams and fears. We already read so much into his life and his last days; why not his last game of racquetball?

On Loitering:
The Mosquito started it. I was innocently doing research on what I thought of as "morally" significant sound or noise, thinking about how sound can be used to hurt someone. I stumbled across

the Moving Sound Technologies website and discovered the Mosquito, an anti-loitering device using sound waves that can only be heard by humans between the ages of thirteen and twenty-five. The device emits a high-pitched signal that is annoying and irritating to this specific age group. It's used regularly to prevent loitering and loitering-related crimes such as vandalism, drug dealing, and prostitution. This is a new kind of sound warfare, sound as deterrent, and it both intrigued and frightened me a little bit. I'd heard about cell-phone rings that can only be heard by young people but this was something new. It got me thinking about the ethics and politics of public spaces, particularly the way loitering ordinances and laws attempt to legislate the subjectivity of individuals, allowing authorities or common citizens to define intent. Further research into famous arrests for loitering led me to Dr. Martin Luther King, Jr. and the iconic photograph that begins the essay. As I began working on the piece, I also found myself thinking about images that might go along with each section; these photographs were very much part of the process of the essay. I made trips to the Food King and the nearby elementary school to snap shots of their anti-loitering signs with my cell-phone. I started noticing these signs everywhere and I wanted to write the kind of essay that asks a reader to think deeply about something we see everyday, something we overlook or ignore most of the time, and I wanted the reader never to see these signs the same way again. The essay was first published in *The Rumpus* as "On Loitering," but I revised and adapted it a bit for this anthology, adding in the material about Montaigne and changing the title.

It Begins with a Knock at the Door:
Originally published as "Confessions of a Parasite," this essay is, for me, as much about the "writer mind," as it is about anything

else that happens on the page, an idea that is also echoed in the essays "Seven Fathoms Down" and "Crown and Shoulder" or even "All of a Dither," where I'm concerned with the overlap between writing *about* the world and being *in* the world. In this essay I was trying to understand what it means to live in my head much of the time, to think of the world around me and the people I meet every day as possible material or subjects for an essay. I cannot figure out if it makes me a bad person or a good person. But the essay is, of course, also about how one sound, one knock on the door, can radically alter the course of the story you tell yourself, how it can force you out of your head and into action and engagement with real pain. So it's also about how I have trouble moving between the interiority of my mind, my writing projects, into the exteriority of interacting with real live vulnerable human beings. The essay also connects back to the title essay "Ultrasonic" since the experiences in it bookended our time in Madrid.

Playlist for Finishing a Book:
This piece was written first as an annotated playlist for the *Largehearted Boy* website as part of their "Book Notes" series where an author creates a playlist that is somehow connected to his/her forthcoming book. I had a lot fun doing it. But I didn't think much of it for a while after it was published. These songs fueled much of my writing and revision process for my last book *The Day After The Day After: My Atomic Angst* and are near and dear to my heart for reasons that are, perhaps, largely sentimental and nostalgic. It wasn't until I started chasing down research on "morally relevant sound" for this book that the songs came back to me in a new way. I stumbled across a list of the top ten songs used by interrogators from the United States to psychologically break down and torture detainees and, though it perhaps isn't a

surprise, I was still troubled to realize that many of my favorite songs and artists are on that list. I had a hard time making sense of what it might mean, if anything, that I love the same songs people I find morally abhorrent use for evil purposes. Of course I realize these are songs millions of Americans love. Though it's not the mission of this essay (or perhaps any essay) to come to an easy conclusion, the piece became an effort to explore my own culpability (albeit somewhat obliquely) for my country's practice of torture while also trying to suggest that, at least for me, there is something in my role as a father that brings these questions into a different sort of focus, complicating the lens I've been constructing for myself as a writer and a parent.

PERSONAL ACKNOWLEDGEMENTS

This book could not have been written without the support and guidance of a great many friends, family, colleagues, editors, and students. For inspiring me and challenging me and for enriching my life in so many ways, thank you to my children, Malcolm and Sophia; and thank you to my family, Sally and John Ramage, Ed and Carolyn Church, Cory Church, and my brother, Matthew Church, as well as my step-siblings, Chris and Laura Ramage, the Ramage and Mele families, and Rob Shufelt for all of their continued support. Many thanks also to Rachel Church. I also owe a debt of gratitude to all the editors and staff at the literary magazines where these essays were first published; and I am especially grateful for my partners, my dear friends and co-editors of the literary magazine, *The Normal School*, Sophie Beck, Matt Roberts, and our Editor-at-Large, Adam Braver. I'm also lucky to work with incredible students and dynamite colleagues in the MFA Program at Fresno State—Randa Jarrar, Corrine Hales, John Hales, Tim Skeen, and Alex Espinoza. I owe a particularly huge debt of gratitude to Vida Samiian, the Dean of the College of Arts and Humanities from 2004-2014 and the best advocate any writer/teacher could ever hope to have. Thanks to Fresno State, the Department of English, the College of Arts and Humanities and my many fine colleagues for their support. Thanks also to other amazing writers and friends around the country who have helped with this book in one way or another--Dinty W. Moore, Patrick Madden, Joe Bonomo, Lia Purpura, Elena Passarello, Justin Hocking, Matthew Gavin Frank, Edwidge Danticat, Nicole Walker, Ander Monson, Roxane Gay, Marcia Aldrich, Billy Giraldi, Sven Birkets, William Bradley, Kirk Wisland, Liz

Scheid, Christopher Spiker, Robert Atwan, and many many others. Thank you to Petra Meyer-Frazier for her copyediting and Kristen Radtke for her beautiful cover design; and thanks to Bill Lavender, editor and friend, without whom none of this would be possible. Finally I owe more than thanks or words for the support and inspiration of Andrea Mele, who has helped me talk, think, and write my way through many of these essays.

Made in the USA
San Bernardino, CA
05 July 2017